To Kate,

Enjoy the read, and Practice,
Practice, Practice.

"Driver's Ed Bill"
Bill Mueller

9-14-23

Come Drive
With Me!

Praise for *"Come Drive With Me!"*

"Bill Mueller's collection of on-the-road anecdotes and wisdom gained from a career in education offer not only a delightful read but valuable insights for soon-to-be motorists and their parents."

—Doug Melvold, Publisher Emeritus
Maquoketa Sentinel-Press and Bellevue Herald-Leader, Iowa

"Bill has taught for 40 years, 10 of these in a driver's ed car. He has a unique and fun perspective of the teen driver. You will love this drive with his tips and anecdotes."

—Al Tubbs, Ph.D., Chairman & CEO
Ohnward Bancshares, Inc.

"Bill Mueller is a life-long educator who is committed to sharing the joy brought to his life through serving as a driver's education teacher. His words of wisdom match timeless safe driving advice with the unique humor found by teaching teens to drive."

—Jane Schmidt, 2014 Iowa Teacher of the Year
Director of Professional Growth & Student Learning
Maquoketa Community Schools, Maquoketa, Iowa

"I would recommend this work to you as a presentation of the importance of becoming, and being, a responsible traveler on our public highways. And, even better, it is told in an easy-to-follow format, well sprinkled with Bill's good humor, as he describes his real-life experiences as a teacher of prospective drivers, together with his observations of human nature. It is bound to hold your interest throughout. I would recommend this presentation

Praise for *"Come Drive With Me!"*

to anyone who has, or who aspires, to sit behind the wheel of the modern automobile. There is still so much that can be learned."

—Asher Schroeder, Assistant U.S. Attorney, Retired
Northern Iowa District

"Bill Mueller uses a blended format by incorporating humor and storytelling to share some important lessons about one of the great 'common experiences' in American culture... learning to drive. Very well done!"

—Dr. Kim P. Huckstadt, Superintendent, Retired
Maquoketa Community Schools, Maquoketa, Iowa

"A compilation of facts and funny musings from a veteran driver's ed instructor."

—Bill Homrighausen, Author
"They Call Me Mr. DeWitt"

"I believe being a driver education teacher is one of the toughest occupations to have. Bringing levity to that world is worth the reading. The old saying that you cannot judge a book by its cover is false in this case. You will enjoy the content throughout, as there are many funny stories told."

—Pat "Flash" Flanagan
Loras College Varsity Athletic Hall of Fame Member

Come Drive With Me!

The Adventures, Perils, and Insights of a Driver's Ed Instructor

Bill Mueller

DeWitt, Iowa

Cover, dingbats, and chapter illustrations were created by Audrey Mueller. The car dingbat separates different stories, and the owl dingbat indicates history, facts, and tips.

If you have any questions or want to share any stories, feel free to contact the author at the email above, or at this official website: www.driversedbill.com

Names of students and parents and others involved in these stories have all been changed, with the exception of Bill Mueller's brothers and sisters and children.

Readers should be aware that internet sites offered as citations and/or sources for further information may have changed or disappeared between the time of this writing and when it is read.

The author has taken liberties with the State of Iowa Department of Transportation term "driver education" used in the official Driver's Handbook. Throughout this book, he has often used the more informal term "driver's ed" as the colloquial nickname everyone uses for driver education.

Table of Contents

Table of Contents

There is no scientific reason for the selections of chapters in this book. It is not a textbook, and these pages do not contain all the answers. They do take an enjoyable and common-sense look at many of the frequent and challenging aspects of driving.

Preface

When I retired from full time teaching five-and-a-half years ago, I told everyone I was going to write a book. So I continued teaching driver education part-time and started recording stories. My wife, Audrey, and I plan our frequent travel around my driver's ed schedule.

Volunteering was also an avenue I wanted to pursue. I thought it might be fun to read to elementary students, but that would require a strict schedule. I had just freed myself from one of those. I tried donating time at a local nursing home. I knew almost immediately that wasn't my calling.

I have always enjoyed teaching, working with teens, and telling stories. I decided the best way for me to use my talent and serve others would be to give driving talks. I came up with "Come Drive With Me: The Adventures, Perils, and Insights of a Driver's Ed Instructor!" This is a fun 30- to 45-minute presentation that is entertaining, educational, and easy to follow. I share much laughter along with many suggestions to help make driving both easier and safer for all.

I speak mainly to civic and senior groups. I have also spoken at Iowa's State Driver Education Conference, and at a Rockwell Collins safety meeting in Bellevue, Iowa, both of which had 150 attendees. To date, I have given 18 talks, with 19 and 20 already scheduled.

Meanwhile, I continued to write and I took three online writing courses. About a year-and-a-half ago, I ran into Christine Gilroy, whom I have known for almost 20 years. She was the 2011 Iowa Journalism Teacher of the Year, Rod Vahl Award winner. She taught high school English and advised the Central DeWitt High School newspaper and yearbook for 23 years. Christine, newly retired, is helping local authors publish their books. She was the answer I had been praying for.

Audrey agreed to illustrate my book and draw the dingbats, those little cars and owls you see throughout the book. For her, this was much more enjoyable than fixing sentences and paragraphs, for which I needed a lot of help. It has been fun working together watching my dream progress from just written notes in a spiral notebook to a finished product.

I hope you love this book and share it with all your family and friends.

—Driver's Ed Bill

Acknowledgments

I thank God for my opportunities and His blessings.

I would like to thank my wife, Audrey, for her love, patience, support, and creativity these past 39 years. Audrey illustrated the cover, the car and owl dingbats, and the chapter drawings. I appreciate her ability to visualize, as well as the talent she has to put these fun images on paper. Audrey, thank you for helping to bring my stories to life.

Thanks to Dad and Mom, Edwin "Red" and Marcella Mueller, for the lessons they taught. From Dad we learned how to work, be responsible, and appreciate a good story. Mom taught her children and grandchildren how to love and serve others while thoroughly enjoying the trip through life.

My children and their families—Whitney Jost and her husband, Bob; Tyler and his wife, Samantha; and Marcy—have been a wealth of encouragement and stories they participated in.

Coming from a big farm family, I found that my brothers and sisters, especially Mark, Jane, and Mike, were a great source of material and encouragement.

Thanks to friends, fellow driver education instructors, acquaintances, and students who lived these adventures and kindly shared their experiences in these 290-plus stories.

I believe God sent Christine Gilroy to edit my work and to lead Audrey and me through the maze of details that were necessary to make one of my dreams become reality.

To Merlyn Usher, now gone, my friend, coach, and guide for more than thirty years.

To John McLean, "Uncle John" to my kids. He has been a brother for four decades.

—Driver's Ed Bill

Come Drive With Me!

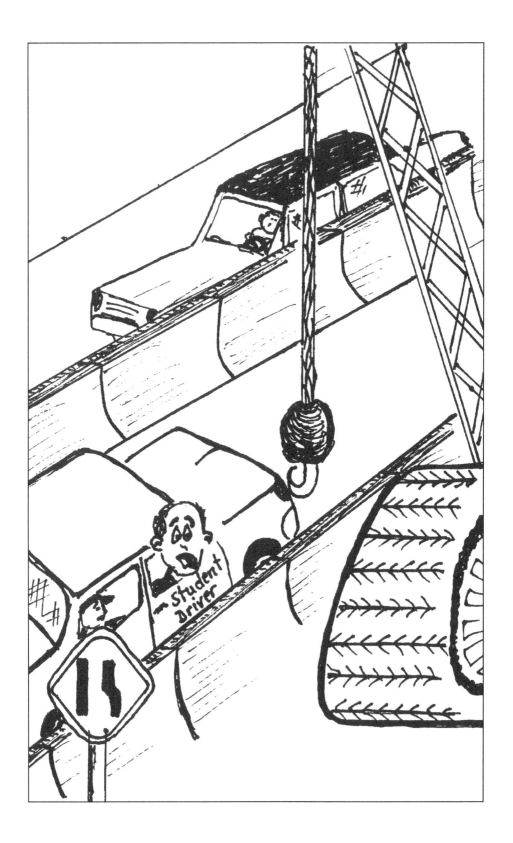

Chapter 1: Passenger Insights

Learning To Drive

The assistant manager of Casey's calls me "The Bravest Man in America." She sees me frequently switching drivers at the convenience store. I often tell people that after 34 years of teaching 8th graders, I was ready for a change. I needed something safer and less stressful, so I became an instructor for what we all call driver's ed, which the state officially calls driver education. It is funny the reaction I get from frightened parents who have a child getting close to driver's permit land. They will ask, "How could you ever do that?" My response is, "Some people get their adrenaline rush with extreme sports. I just get mine every time I get in a driver's ed car."

Ray tells about his second son at 16. He wasn't that interested in driving, so he wouldn't study for the written permit test. They drove to the driving station 30 minutes to Clinton so often that the examiners all knew both of them by first name. That young man is now a junior at Ashford University in Clinton. He has a 20-year old girlfriend from Chicago with no license and no interest in learning. Ray tells about getting his own license at 16 with permission to date, also. One of his first opportunities was a double date with a kid down the street. They picked up Ray's girl then had a 15-mile drive to get his buddy's date. Out on the highway the car killed several times. Each time they got it started and limped a ways before the engine would die again. After three or four times, Ray's date leaned over and said, "I thought this was supposed to happen on the way home."

was always critical of Donald's driving scores, even though he would never let him practice.

Donald was both the class clown and the know-it-all. He was immature for a senior, and annoying to Officer Lansing, our first guest speaker. He made observations or asked questions for which he didn't want answers. The next drive after that presentation, Donald randomly asked if I had any favorite sayings. I told him, "Check the fruit on the tree," explaining if someone was an expert then you shut up, listen and learn what you can. He had no idea I was talking about him and his behavior toward Officer Lansing. When our next guest speaker came from the Department of Transportation, I limited him to four comments or questions. In that class he didn't say anything. On one of our drives he told me, "This music sucks." It was oldies we listened to in the car. I told him, "Tough." I didn't argue or take it personally.

In Iowa, once a student completes driver's education and demonstrates the proper skills and knowledge, he or she can get a driver's license without taking a DOT drive test. I told Donald he was not ready to drive by himself. He was going to have to take the drive test at the driving station. He was more subdued than usual. I suggested he take the drive test in Maquoketa. With less traffic, it would be easier. Also, once he had the 20 hours of practice that is required to get his license, the test would be a breeze.

Thomas was one of the best student drivers I have worked with. He was from the Bahamas and lived with an aunt and uncle. Because he is very good in math, he is considering either engineering or actuary science for a career. As social as Thomas is, I question whether he will be able spend his life working in a cubicle. He is considering attending either Iowa State University or the University of Iowa. When his mother back home learned that UI was selected the 2013 party school of the year[1], she started lobbying for him to attend Iowa State.

Two brothers, Logan and Hunter, both had little driving experience. Dad started driving with the boys once class started, and they improved rapidly, as most students do when they drive. Hunter was a junior, quiet, but usually he had good questions and observations. Logan, a sophomore, talked only when he had an excuse or a complaint, a typical behavior for frustrated students. He was more interested in each drive's score than in any improvement.

Liv was almost 17. She had no hobbies or interests. Her mother placed her in driver's ed without her permission. Her attitude was as poor as her driving ability. Up until now she has refused to drive with Mom or anyone else.

Sofie blew off one of her drives. I reached her with the second phone number I was given. She claimed she had to babysit and wouldn't make it. This was odd, because generally, good drivers don't skip.

Tate was a talkative and likeable kid. His challenge was staying focused while driving. He hadn't driven a lot and was on the DOT drive test bubble. On his last drive, because of heavy traffic, we had difficulty getting into the proper lane returning to school. Instead we turned into the Quick Stop station across the street. While turning around with his drive almost complete, he accidentally punched the gas pedal instead of the brake. My stomping the dual brake prevented us from damaging the car and the parking stump and taking out the bushes beyond. Tate was devastated. I decided to take him and a friend out for 15 more minutes of driving after our last class Tuesday night. He drove well and didn't have to drive with the DOT.

Iowa and South Dakota are the only two states that allow 14-year-olds to drive.[2] Upon passing a written test in Iowa, 14-year-olds may take driver education. After successfully completing the course and waiting six months, they can get a school permit, which has rigid guidelines and strict sanctions for disobeying the rules.

Arguments against 14-year-old drivers include immaturity, narrow peripheral vision, and poor time-space judgment. I have worked with many students age 14 to 18 not ready to drive. Some lack maturity; for others it's poor focus and lack of motor-processing, cognitive and biomechanical skills. Parents are responsible for determining the readiness of their child. Parents should be applauded for making their children wait if they are deficient in any of the above areas. Practice is key. With practice you improve. Can you imagine performing for a music recital with an instrument you have never played? How about winning a game for which you have never trained? Sometimes when students make a mistake, they say, "I'm sorry." I tell them not to apologize, because I know they are doing their best with the experience they have. As their skills improve, the more confident they become and eventually the driving task becomes enjoyable.

Driver's License

Like magic, your license gave you the independence and mobility you always longed for. Now you were able to go places and accomplish tasks without having to rely on others.

One excited girl slid in the driver's seat, looked over at me, smiled, and said, "This is the first time I have ever sat behind the steering wheel of a car."

A friend told me of her drive partner, who had never driven before. When their instructor gave her the keys, she had no idea where to even put them to start the car.

Ellen's father was a successful manager of a prominent business in town. She was not ready to drive. On her third drive she scored a 36%. That was a gift. This was after three hours practicing in the parking lot. You might ask what happens when you take drivers out of the lot too soon? They drive up on the sidewalk. Joggers, be vigilant. I called her father for the third time, finally convincing him she should be pulled from the class. Unfortunately, I didn't have a camera for this Kodak moment when I informed Jane that Ellen, her drive partner, had dropped the class.

Sheer *relief* spread across her face when she realized she would live to see her 16th birthday. Priceless. Ellen took driver education the following year and passed. She had a crash the first week with her license.

The first thing many foreign exchange students do upon arriving in Iowa is sign up for driver education class. I have taught teens from China, Germany, Norway, Sweden, and the Bahamas. Each country has a different driver education cost. Several foreign exchange students have shared with me the cost of getting licensed in their home countries. It ranges from $2,500 to $5,000.

My daughter Marcy spent a semester studying in a European country. She thought maybe she would meet a nice guy there. She discovered many of the young men have no license, no job and are alcoholics. It was on to plan B for Marcy.

Sam told the following stories. In 1949, he watched his older sister Alice one week after getting her driver's license. She backed into a big tree at the end of their long country lane. Upset after surveying the damage to both car and tree, Alice took out her license, ripped it up, and to this day has never driven again.

Years later, with two small children, Sam and his wife, Florence, decided she should get her driver's license. After appropriate practice they felt she was ready. Sam was going to watch the kids while the state trooper took Mom out for her drive test. Because the kids would fuss without Mom, the officer reluctantly allowed Dad and the children to ride quietly in the back seat. Except for parking the car along the street, Florence was finished with her test, when suddenly the calm broke. Just as abruptly the trooper decided Alice didn't need to finish as originally planned. She passed without parking and has been driving ever since.

A miracle occurred a couple of years ago. One of my students drove only twice before she started driver education. She was 16 and a quick learner. On her fifth and sixth drives with me she scored a 100%. In 10 years, with several thousand hours, this had never happened before. These were great scores, but she is still at risk because of her lack of driving experience.

In 1901, New York first registered automobiles. Chicago issued license buttons that drivers wore while behind the wheel. In 1918, all states required license plates on autos. In 1956, license plates became a standard size.

By the 1930s, many high schools offered driver education. Before that, people were taught to drive by salesmen, family, friends, and at the YMCA. By 1939 only 39 states required a driver's license for Americans.[3] If you are going to let your teen get a driver's license, experience is the most important gift you will ever give them. Parents put their children in real danger if they allow them to get a license without the needed practice. Research concludes that it takes about five years for most novices to become proficient at the driving task."[4]

We have some students coming to driver education with little or zero experience. A reluctant parent can start practicing with the teen in a large parking lot, and increase difficulty of the drive as the teen's skills and confidence improve. If you are afraid to drive with your teen, find someone who will. Do you have a spouse, parent, sibling, or family friend who will help you out?

Students who have practiced a lot find that driving in the driver education car is much more enjoyable than they had anticipated. Some students are nervous and unfamiliar with the car, and their first drive isn't the best. Some parents won't drive with their teenager, so the student knows his or her skills are poor. When their frustration increases, they sometimes argue with me. When this happens I ask, "Would you like your driver education experience to be pleasant or unpleasant?" They say, "Pleasant." So I reply, "Then don't argue with me."

I also tell them to practice at least two hours before our next drive. It is amazing how much most students improve in that time. The older the student, usually the more quickly he or she will learn. I also offer to call parents if the student thinks it will actually help get more driving time.

If you have ever worked with a beginner, these situations will sound familiar. You stomped on the imaginary brake every time your driver was going to rear-end the car ahead at the light. Numerous times you freaked out when you thought your driver was going to run the stop sign or sideswipe a parked car. You were certain you were going to meet your Lord when your driver pulled out in front of an 18-wheeler. Or how about the times you sat, and sat, waiting to pull out?

New drivers don't do stupid things while driving with parents on purpose. They haven't yet learned how to judge time and distance. One speaker explained it takes about 20 hours of practice for most 14-year-olds to get it. The older the students are, usually the faster they learn. But not always.

Education

Craig admitted, "It was pretty humbling when I realized I wasn't the pro I thought I was." He is an old college friend who lives in Lincoln, Neb. He tells about teaching his two boys how to drive. The first was raring to go and learned quickly. With his initial success, Craig was pretty confident in his ability to teach son No. 2, but Hank wasn't as eager and didn't have the early skills demonstrated by his older brother. Craig soon learned his first father-son success was dumb luck.

Craig shared the following experience he had with Hank driving through a construction site: Instead of the traditional orange cones to designate out of bounds, the workers had set up a line of 24-four-inch high, 1.5-inch white PVC pipes topped with orange ribbons, which I guess are cheaper to replace than the big orange cones. Hank, driving too fast and unable to keep his car centered in the lane, proceeded to mow down the whole line of markers.

Bo from West Des Moines, another college friend, tells about his 16-year old daughter Caitlin's first two mishaps. Not paying attention, she rear-ended another car at a stop sign. Then she was hit by another young driver experiencing her first winter behind the wheel.

This girl was trying to pull out from her driveway, and the view was obstructed by mountains of snow everywhere. Too impatient to wait, she decided she was just going to pull out and hope for the best. This resulted in her T-boning Caitlin's car.

Woodrow is a laid-back 65-year-old driving instructor. This August, one of his students shared with him, "My brother said I should be prepared to be hollered at a lot by my driving instructor. You haven't hollered at all."

I would be curious to know who his brother's screaming teacher had been. I am certain it was someone who was not fulfilled spending summer days in a car with novice drivers.

My sister-in-law grew up in an area where private companies taught all driver education classes. The firm she learned from was a family-owned business. The teachers were a father, his son, and daughter-in-law. She said the son was a "player," meaning he wasn't faithful.

When students drove with him, he would stop at various places to flirt with the high school girls. His wife was all business and would quiz the teens where they had driven. She was really looking for more information than was prudent for them to share.

Louie took driver education in DeWitt in the mid-1960s. Mr. Nick Predney was his instructor. Nick said that in 30 years, Louie was the only student driver who ever got picked up by the police in his driver's education car. He only got a warning that time.

In that era, classes were taught as part of the school-day curriculum. Coming back from Lowden, Nick misjudged the time of their return. Between Calamus and Grand Mound there was a clear stretch of road. The car was a Plymouth Fury; it had a 383 magnum with four on the floor. Back then, students were required to learn how to drive a standard transmission. Not wanting to be late for the next class, Mr. Predney told Louie to give it the gas, which he did, not noticing the police car behind. The officer pulled them over and approached the car. At that time, cars had only lap belts. With difficulty, Louie tried to reach for his permit. Mr. Predney said, "Unbuckle your seat belt; it will be much easier to get at your wallet."

In one session I had drivers collectively the worst I had ever seen in 10 years as an instructor. It was the second drive for all of them. We went to Anamosa, our easiest drive, with its numerous rolling hills and mild curves. If these students didn't improve, seven of the nine drivers were going to have to take the drive test. Their scores were two A's, one low B, three C's, one D, and two F's.

Most of these students didn't see potential hazards, stop signs, or speed limit signs. They approached stops signs too fast and then rolled through them. Some were way too cautious. They struggled to keep a consistent speed and were guilty of speeding, weaving and overcorrecting, and driving on the both the centerline and the white fog line next to the shoulder.

Geno got his permit March 27 and started driver education class April 27. After his third of six drives, I called his Mom to encourage her to drive with him. At this point he had two graded drives, a 51% and a 66%. She said, "I think you're too intimidating to Geno. His Dad has driven with him and thinks his driving isn't that bad." I couldn't tell her that the two girls who had been his drive partners were both hoping they'd live to see the end of the school year when he drove.

On his fourth drive, Geno explained, "I drive with Dad, but Mom freaks out and refuses to get in the car with me." This time he scored a 61%. Driving north on Brady, a four-lane street in Davenport, I said, "We will have to change lanes." Without looking, he jerked the wheel, almost hitting the red sedan on our left front quarter panel. The car wasn't even in our blind spot. Earlier in the session, Geno had injured his arm in physical education class and missed one drive. I was thinking, Good, this will give him more time to practice. His drive partner finished a couple of days before he did, so on his last drive he was alone and we needed a third person to ride along. I asked Mom to come with us. I thought this would be a great opportunity to have her to see how dangerous Geno really was. She said, "No I can't, I am busy, but I will line up someone to go." Another relative agreed to be our rider while Grandma babysat her two children.

His final drive grade was a D+. I explained to him that he wasn't ready to drive by himself, and he would be required to take the drive test at the driving station. This was okay, because he understood he needed a lot more practice. Though Geno was already 16 he would have to wait until next March to get his intermediate license. Since 2014 the Iowa requires teens under age 18 to have their instruction permit for 12 months before they will be allowed to get an intermediate license. Good job,

Iowa Legislature. This will give him almost a year to practice. Maybe by that time Mom will be willing to ride with him.

I had a group of five boys a couple of years ago. All of them were nice. Two were very smart. None were very interested in having a driver's license. I asked, "Why are you spending the time and money to take driver education?" They said they were 15 and 16 and their parents thought it would be a good idea for them to have a license. At home these teens had no responsibilities and nothing was expected of them. All their parents wanted was for them to stay out of trouble and graduate from high school.

These guys had no ambition, dreams, or goals for their lives. All of their spare time was spent playing video games or hacky-sack. They weren't being taught any of the skills necessary to become independent, productive contributors in our society. They will all receive their high school diploma, but I pray they won't still be living at home when they are 35. I hope Mom and Dad won't have to raise the grandchildren.

 One of these boys had a younger sister who took driver's education eight months later. Cindy wanted out. She was a good student, a hard worker with a job. She had plans for a car, career, and a future. Her No. 1 goal was to be nothing like her senior brother and his best friend. According to her, they were barely meeting the requirements to graduate. Neither was driving because they both were too lazy to find a job, which would pay for a car, insurance, and the gasoline to go in it.

Contrast that story with teenagers who come from an Amish Mennonite community of 13 families in our area. Even though their formal education ends after eighth grade, they are still required to take driver's education if they get a driver's license before age 18. Their religion requires that their pictures not be taken close up. The permit reads, "Valid Without Photo." Their lifestyle resembles the Amish in dress, children's education, religion, social customs, and work ethic, but the difference is that the Mennonites drive vehicles and use electricity, power tools, telephones, and modern technology.

To date, I have taught eight of their kids, and I was delighted to meet them and their parents. This is a group who moved to Jackson County for better opportunities. The first families arrived just a few years ago.

One February I drove with two brothers, Adam, 16, and Peter, 14. Both were serious drivers who had practiced a lot. They were very polite and personable. Adam was much more talkative. Any time he didn't know an answer he would always defer to Peter.

The boys' Dad built a chicken barn with a length of more than 500 feet. It houses more than 23,000 birds. The boys referred to the chickens as "layers." They produce organic eggs. They had a young flock, not yet fully matured. Each batch of chickens lays for 13 months then is replaced at $7.50 a bird, quite an investment. There are no chemicals added in any phase of the operation. The birds are all on the ground in a building that is state of the art. Did you know Iowa is the top egg-producing state in America?

The family also breeds Devon cattle, which originated in England. These are grass-fed beef of a dark red color. These, too, are also raised organically. These Mennonites use the most modern computer technology, including embryo transplants and pasture rotation multiple times daily. Their farm is 200 acres of hilly ground, plus they rent 40 more. Hay and pasture are the only crops they grow. All the chicken feed is bought.

Mennonites don't listen to the radio, watch television, or see movies. After purchasing their vehicles, they disable the radio. Adam even asked me what a movie was. Have you ever tried to explain to a 16-year-old what a movie is? Their family travels and vacations frequently. They have seen documentaries in museums they have visited.

Mennonites, unlike the Amish, can live some distance from the community church and school. The adults all drive. Some of these families lived up to 12 miles away.

Their Sunday services are about two hours in length. If a member sins, or misbehaves, he repents, then is accepted back into the church. My two students asked me, "How do other people repent?" I told the boys many people don't attend church and aren't part of any congregation. Many people would have to go to Webster's Dictionary to even know what *repent* meant, as Adam was asking.

The boys had an accent. They explained that at home their families speak German, since they were originally from Switzerland, the boys thought. They start school in first grade and begin to learn English. All school materials and instruction are in English. The children are bilingual and by age 14, all are fluent in two languages.

John, the father, invited me to visit their family's farm. My wife, Audrey, grew up on a big Wisconsin dairy farm where they raised 6,000 laying hens. I was anxious to see a modern egg facility, owned and operated by the most conservative people I have ever met. In August, Audrey, our two daughters, son-in-law, grandson and I visited. We spent a fun hour learning about modern egg production. The chicken barn and equipment were fascinating. We ran out of time and didn't even get to see the cattle. They sent us home with some grass-fed hamburger, steaks, and pullet eggs. That fall I had six more Mennonite students and I learned more about their community. All the families moved from Arkansas or Illinois, and they are all related at some point. Most are self-employed farmers. Six of these families raise eggs. Three use organic methods, the others don't. Frances was 16 and identical twins Ron and Roy almost 15. In my class of 23, they were the top three students. Their Dad owned his own lawn service and was a self-employed carpenter.

I also had Beth, 15, her sister Mary, newly 14, and Will, 15. Both of their families own egg farms. Their mothers are sisters, making them first cousins. They also were excellent students. These six students were in the top nine in the whole class, even though formal education for them ends after completing eighth grade. The girls wear bonnets and long skirts. The boys all wear a hat.

The Mennonites were as curious about the high school as everyone else was about their new classmates. This driver's ed class was the model of diversity. All were respectful and worked well together throughout the course. A year-and-a-half before, the twins with their family had moved from Arkansas. They enjoy Iowa's winter, because it allows them to play hockey about once a week.

In September Will's older sister married Adam and Peter's brother Charles. Several hundred people attended the wedding. Most of the guests came from Illinois and Arkansas.

I met Ginny from New Jersey, where insurance rates are through the roof. She was still in her 20s and said by taking a driving course every so often she got a 15 percent discount on her insurance. In rural Iowa, these types of courses are for drivers over 50 years of age and the discounts are almost nothing. There is no incentive for anyone to become a better driver. I wish Iowa would offer an optional eight-hour refresher course for all adults over 25. People develop a lot of bad habits, which only get worse with years of driving with no help or advice. In Iowa, at age 70 you must renew your license every two years.

Sometimes I am asked, "How can you teach driver education?"

The instructor in one of my certification courses told us, "Teaching driver education is the most important class we will ever teach. Some of the lessons our students learn may save their lives." This message I have taken to heart, spending many extra hours each session preparing my students to be safe young drivers.

I also enjoy the variety in my students. My 20 drivers from my last class had parents, grandparents, or cousins from eight countries—Canada, England, Germany, India, Portugal, Thailand, and Vietnam. Some of the parents migrated to Iowa from 12 other states—Alabama, California, Hawaii, Illinois, Kansas, Louisiana, Michigan, Missouri, Oklahoma, Texas, Virginia, and Wisconsin. In addition to all the school sports represented, I had a student trainer, ski team performer, professional musician, and participants in karate, drama, forensics, theater, and competitive cheer. Several had jobs, and a boy and girl even played Sheepshead, the German card game that I love to play.

During two days in the same week we had three close calls. First was a boy without much highway driving experience who dropped the right wheels down onto the shoulder of the road at 50 mph. The county maintenance people hadn't been there yet to fill the six-inch deep gully next to the pavement. I grabbed the wheel, then calmly said, "Take your foot off the gas." Once the shoulder came back up to the level of the concrete, we moved back onto the highway and proceeded on our way. In that same area north of Princeton, Iowa, we had someone pass us with an oncoming car no more than 50 yards away. I slammed on our brake, and the driver of the oncoming car hit the shoulder and the brake, avoiding a head-on collision.

The next day we attempted to enter Interstate 80 from the Interstate 74 ramp going east. Inexperienced Angel was driving too slowly, not the suggested 40-45 mph coming off a cloverleaf.

With heavy traffic, the semi in the next lane wasn't able to move over. He tried to reduce his speed to let us in, but with his size and weight it was impossible to match the 30-35 mph that we were traveling. Once again, I grabbed the wheel and we drove down the shoulder until a space opened for us to merge safely.

For the driver with zero experience, my first instructions are pretty basic. "This is a steering wheel; the pedal on the left is the brake; the accelerator, called the gas pedal, is on the right." I don't grade our first drive lesson, because sometimes students are nervous and it takes them a while to get used to the car and me. I do write comments, so they know where to make improvements. Each driver gets a copy after every session.

When giving my talks or writing my stories, my goal is to entertain while teaching. I share true events I didn't or couldn't make up. With more knowledge and some reflection, we can all be more patient, improved drivers. The most dangerous thing we do each day is get into a car.

In 1990 the U.S. population was 254,506,647 with 44,599 highway deaths.[5] In 2010 our population was 312,247,116, up almost 20%, with 33,808 deaths, down 24%.[6] The federal, state, and local governments have improved our streets and highways. Automakers have done their part and added numerous improvements and safety features on their cars. Unfortunately, since cell phone technology has been invented, we are now seeing fatality rates turn upward nationwide once again. A new study reviewed 180 fatal crashes in which cell phone use was the suspected cause, but only half of these cases actually reported distracted driving as the cause.[7]

I learned a couple of years ago that the Iowa DOT tracks all teen fatalities in the state and institutes a special high school program in areas with the highest death rates. In 2012, at the State Driver Education Conference, we listened to a speaker from another state. Residents of her state believed driver education wasn't necessary. Some thought parents alone were capable of preparing their teens for the road. As she put it, "When the bodies started piling up like cordwood, the state reinstated driver education."

Driver education is no longer mandatory after a person reaches age 18. Some young people are waiting until then to get a driver's license. For the 18- to 24-year-old age group, fatalities nationwide are on the rise.

Driver education was first taught in schools back in the 1930s. I grew up in Wisconsin where state-required instruction was not mandatory until 1969. This was the year I turned 16.

For most teenagers in Iowa, 16 is still considered the magic age. They can get a driver's license, which gives them mobility and freedom. You might wonder, "Why doesn't everyone get a license at 16?" There are several reasons. For some parents, the cost of driver education, a vehicle, and insurance are real financial burdens. Other parents are too scared and refuse to drive with their children. Some teens don't have the motor skills or processing skills they need to drive successfully. There are parents who, though they have tried, realize the only chance their child is going to have is to get professional instruction through a driver education class offering. Some teens are afraid or lazy—they would rather play with their phones or video games. This last group is usually kids who are uninvolved in school, church, or community activities.

The two major problems with not taking a certified driving course are that many young drivers will not have been taught properly and will not have the hours of driving practice they need. In Iowa, students are supposed to have 20 hours of practice before they can get their school or intermediate license.

Young people without much drive time are at the highest risk. We sometimes have parents putting their kids in a driver education car with little or zero experience. With practice, most teens improve quickly. The older they are, usually the faster they learn.

In Iowa, if a student doesn't have the skills to drive alone, he or she must take the drive test at the driving station with a DOT examiner. I determine this by the average drive grade. If they score below an 80% after six hours, the drive test is required. Usually 8 to 10% of my students are required to take the drive test because they haven't driven enough to develop the necessary skills.

Practice and wearing seatbelts are the best deterrents to teen fatalities.

Drive Test

Ethel, age 85, told of her drive test experience. Her husband, Gary, taught her how to drive after they were married. Her first drive test was cancelled by a blizzard. At her rescheduled appointment, the driving examiner asked if she had tire chains. Gary quickly borrowed a pair, and they were off. She passed. Sixty years later while driving to Iowa City, she asked, "How is my driving?" Gary's response was, "You drive well. You had a good teacher."

A farm kid, Glen, is now 75. Alone, he drove himself down to the police station to take his drive test. Upon passing, he drove himself home. Different times back then.

One time, my wife, Audrey, was practicing with one of her special needs students. We let her use our car for the drive test. Though Lena was driving poorly, she went to take the drive test anyway. Lena returned to the car sooner than Audrey had expected. When questioned, she explained to Audrey that she was legally blind and failed the eye test—the reason they weren't having much success with her drive lessons.

Kevin, another special needs instructor, was almost killed when helping a student practice for his drive test. I tell about that story in Chapter 2.

After these two harrowing experiences, officials decided it was just too dangerous and too big a liability to teach students in their personal cars. To Audrey's relief, they never tried again. These experiences scarred her for life. When our children became of age to drive, Audrey seldom practiced with them.

I met Rod and wife, Rita. He and I are both Loras College alumni. She was a graduate of Clarke College. They graduated in 1972, the spring before I started at Loras. After completing law school, his first job was determined by driving up scenic Highway 52 along the Mississippi River. Bellevue was beautiful so he decided to stay and build his life and law career in Jackson County.

Rod told about his mother crashing during her drive test. After more practice she passed on her second attempt. His Mom never drove again. Ironically, she was able to teach all of her children to drive because she kept her license valid until she entered the nursing home nine years ago.

I grew up on a farm in Kenosha, Wis., where all young drivers are required to pass a drive test to obtain a license. I have 10 siblings and most of our driving practice was with Mom. She had more success with some than with others. Dad was either at work or doing his own farming at home. My one brother shared his 1960s story. I was amazed that 50 years later his recollection is so vivid.

I barely remember anything about getting my license.

For him, like most 16-year-olds, receiving a driver's license was the most important event in the world, but I guess having to take the drive test four times would be traumatic enough to leave a lasting imprint on anyone's memory.

On his first drive, he reached 40 mph in the parking lot. On his second, Mom screamed every time he got to close to the curb.

He was one of the youngest in his class. Most of his buddies had already been through the tribulations by the time it became his turn. His friends came back with assorted tales of the big, tall, nasty examiner. They all said, "Pray you don't get that guy."

On his first drive test, his examiner told my brother he needed a little more practice. The second time, he got Mr. Intimidation and failed.

On his third try, the car killed a block from the driving station. He and the examiner pushed it into a parking lot and walked back. Because this was his third attempt, he was desperate. He pleaded with the examiner to give him another chance.

My Uncle John, who lived nearby, brought over his brand-new Chrysler Valiant, which my brother Mike later bought. My brother wasn't used to the high performance of this modern car compared with our old Rambler station wagon. Its brakes and gas pedal were pretty touchy.

When they took off, it was much faster than expected. At the first red light, he almost put the examiner through the windshield —no seat belts back then. Angrily, the examiner said, "That's it, we are done."

When they arrived back at the station, Mom asked, "So did he pass?" He did finally pass on his fourth attempt.

Mom had been driving him the eight miles to Saint Catherine's High School for two years, and was anxious for him to drive himself. After finally getting his license, according to Mom, his first question of her was, "How do I get there?" With his great memory, he didn't seem to remember that part of the story. He had me rolling on the floor as he related his woes of a half-century earlier.

My brother Mike was a good driver, but had to take the test twice. He was told that he was a little too cocky.

I was the first in my family required to take driver education. Wisconsin first required the classes in 1969, the year I turned 16. Even with the class, it took me two attempts to get my license. Mark was behind me. He borrowed my Uncle Charlie's standard transmission, and was the first person in our family to pass on the initial attempt. Jane got hers on her first try, also.

Today all fifty states and the District of Columbia have a three- stage Graduated Driver's License system for drivers under the age of 18. Analysis shows that the GDL system will reduce 16- and 17-year-olds' crashes up to 50%.[8]

GDL has three steps: the instruction permit, the intermediate license, and the full license. Each state has its own system for its implementation. Most states do require driver education.

In Iowa, students get 30 hours of classroom instruction and six hours of drive training. In addition, our state requires an added 20 hours of practice behind the wheel. When a student successfully finishes the class, he or she will receive a certificate of completion.

In Iowa, 14-year-olds may take a written test to obtain an instruction permit. This allows them to drive certain hours with proper supervision. After completing driver education and holding a permit for six months, they can get a school license. This comes with many restrictions.

School permit holders must have demonstrated the ability to drive safely. If they haven't, then they get stamped. This means the student must pass a drive test with the examiners at the DOT driving station. They will decide if the student is prepared to drive safely. This is like getting a second opinion before putting young drivers on the road.

When they succeed, school permit holders will be issued an intermediate license, or they may get a school permit if they have not yet qualified for an intermediate license.

A driver who meets all of the requirements and has held a permit for 12 months can get an intermediate license at 16, and 12 months later a full license. Teens should make the upgrade to a full license as soon as possible. If they don't make the upgrade, and they get a ticket, they start all over with the intermediate license. Once a driver turns 18, all of these restrictions no longer apply.

Many people are critical of 14-year-olds behind the wheel. They ask, "Are they mature enough?" Lack of maturity is one reason. The other reason is poor time-space judgment. It takes practice to successfully judge another vehicle's speed and distances traveled.

I have been told the federal government doesn't want 14-year-olds driving. They believe they know what's best for Iowa's young drivers.

I believe Iowa got it right, though. Practice is the key. State Farm's Insurance experts state that a driver is not considered experienced with fewer than 1,000 hours.

When parents act responsibly, 14 is a good age to start driving. I prefer that students practice for two years supervised. In Wisconsin, a teen can't even get behind the wheel until 15-and-a-half, but then the state lets them get a license at 16. I personally do not believe such a short time of supervision gives a young driver the experience needed.

A responsible parent should know when a child is mature enough to drive. Sometimes there are 17-year-olds not ready, and then, some of the best teen drivers are only 14.

Chapter 2: "This is a steering wheel"

Processing Information

Elizabeth, 14, lived with her father in another state. He died suddenly of a heart attack in his 40s. She came to live with her mother. When Mom learned someone else was willing to pay for her daughter's driver education, she decided to enroll her in class.

Elizabeth had good grades in school because she worked hard on her homework each night. She had major processing problems, however, and was no more prepared to drive than a first grader.

Once I told her that we were going to switch drivers up the street at Casey's, which in Iowa are popular gas station convenience stores. As we approached, I instructed Elizabeth, "Put your signal on." She looked at me and said, "Left or right?" She would ask these types of questions at least three times on every drive.

On our last drive, we do a processing thinking-and-driving activity to help students become more independent. They must obey all the traffic laws throughout this drive.

In Maquoketa, we start at the high school on the south end of town. Driver One goes to the Jackson County Fairgrounds on the far northeast side of town. The student is not allowed to make any right turns.

Many streets don't go through, which makes this more challenging for our driver. Once most students figure out the left turns, they can complete the task in 15 to 20 minutes.

When we get to the fairgrounds, it is Driver Two's turn to go back to the high school, this time without making any left turns. Elizabeth wasn't able to find the high school. Plus, she missed one stop sign and a red light, and sat through a green light because she didn't notice it change.

We did this activity one April a few years ago. If Carrie, her drive partner at the time, had not helped her, we would still be driving around looking for the high school.

After each drive, Elizabeth's score hovered between a D and an F. Then she would argue with me. This is a common response for frustrated, inexperienced drivers. These students usually don't get much practice drive time outside of class and they aren't having much success. They don't know what else to do. She did pass the class with a D, but she had her certificate stamped, which meant she would be required to drive with the DOT officials at the driving station to eventually get her license. When she successfully passed her test then she would receive her license.

After our class concluded, I asked her mother what her intentions were. She said, "Elizabeth isn't ready to drive,"—Thanks to you, Mom, I thought,—"but I just wanted to get driver education out of the way. I'm not going to let her get a school permit. She can get her license when she turns 16." How many lives might be at risk, because of this selfish mother? I am sad to report, this is a girl who met all of her driver education requirements, but unfortunately we did not prepare her for the driving world.

As instructors we can't do it alone. Parents need to take a large part of the responsibility in practicing with their sons or daughters.

Bonny was 16. She boasted she had driven 20 times, mostly with her two grown sisters on gravel roads. The first time we got in the car she asked, "Is the gas pedal on the right or left?" She also didn't know enough to depress the brake to shift into gear.

I knew she had lied to me about her driving experience. Her mother was too frightened to get into the vehicle with her and Dad didn't have a license.

We started in a parking lot. The steering wheel was a mystery to her. We spent a few minutes doing figure-eight turns. She seemed to pick that up pretty well. But when we got on a residential street she couldn't focus, losing everything she learned the previous 15 minutes.

When I gave advice she would argue. My usual reply in this circumstance is to ask, while their drive partner is white-knuckling it in the back seat, "Would you like this to be a pleasant experience? Then don't fight me."

I was going to inflate her grade to 50% on our second drive to give her some encouragement. Then she blew the stop sign a half block from our destination. So that score was dashed.

Before our third drive, Bonny boasted having practiced three hours. I did see some improvement until we reached Highway 61, a four-lane divided highway with a 65 mph speed limit. She tried to pull south into two northbound lanes of traffic. Fortunately, I am much stronger and was able to wrestle the wheel from her and pull us into the intersection.

On our fourth drive, I told Bonny, "We are going to turn left at the second stop sign." She never saw the first one. Fortunately, I have a dual brake. Five minutes later we were southbound on South 2nd Street in Clinton. "Okay, after this red light, at the next block, turn right by the big Auto Zone billboard." This time she never saw the red light.

We were going to Davenport and Bettendorf for our fifth drive. She said that was where she usually drove. Leaving the bus barn parking lot she pulled out left, the opposite direction of our route, into two lanes of oncoming traffic going westbound.

Our destination was the roundabout on 53rd Avenue. This is the busiest street in the Quad Cities. With a novice, city traffic is always scary—for me.

Early on this sixth drive, Tyler had gone from the high school tennis courts to Ekstrand Elementary School parking lot without using any right turns. It took 15-20 minutes, the usual time for most drivers. Now it was Bonny's turn to drive from

Ekstrand to the tennis courts not making any left turns. With her focusing difficulties, she couldn't find her way back to the high school and she missed five stop signs on the way.

I called her Dad the next morning, and told him she was going to need at least 20 hours of practice before she took her drive test. He was pleasant to talk to, but he didn't have a license to drive with her. He said he would talk to her. I told him after the recommended drive time I would drive with her free of charge to determine her readiness for a license. I never received a call.

The next week I talked to Eric at the Driver Station, explaining the situation. He asked for her name and said he would be on the lookout for her. Normally I stamp DRIVE TEST REQUIRED in red ink when needed. This time it was in green ink because that was the pen I had. Good thing, for the Driver Station employees would definitely see that!

Josh, 17, another non-processor, explained that he was bipolar and also had an explosive disorder. I wasn't too anxious to remember the technical name for it. He said he erupted violently anytime someone lied to him or when anyone inquired about his father. I was afraid to ask Josh if he would detonate if he didn't pass driver's education.

Some parents see no improvement in their teen's driving, even with practice. They know the young driver is a danger to everyone on the road. As the student gets closer to graduation, they believe a driving instructor is the only hope. Usually they are wrong.

This story is about a responsible mother who did make a sensible decision. Matthew was a student at a neighboring high school. Mom believed it was a requirement for all students to take driver education before graduation. Knowing he wasn't ready, she waited as long as possible.

I had Matthew in June, during one of our summer sessions in Maquoketa. At 17-and-a-half, he was just being allowed by his mother to take the course. His little sister, newly 16, now had her driver's license. He was upset with Mom and didn't understand why she had prevented him from taking driver education sooner. After about 15 seconds in the car with Matt it was pretty obvious. He wasn't ready!

Matthew was very bright with no practical sense. His social skills and cognitive and biomechanical coordination were poor for his age. His brain, hands and feet were not in sync.

Once we were going south on Main Street. When the light turned green, we turned right onto Platt Street. He drove right at a parked pickup truck. I jerked the wheel, preventing a crash and saving our right side view mirror. "We almost hit that parked truck," I said. He retorted with disgust, "That's because I can't multi-task."

I learned that day that turning a corner and not hitting a parked vehicle downtown is sometimes just too much to expect. I hope he never uses a phone while driving.

I saw Matthew 15 months later on a Saturday in September. He was now almost 19. We had pulled into a Casey's gas station to switch drivers. He spotted the driver's education car and then me. Running over he said, "Mr. Mueller! Mr. Mueller, I got my license last week." "What happened?" I asked in surprise. He replied, "It's kind of complicated." I am sorry I didn't think to ask for more details. It would have lengthened this saga by several pages.

In DeWitt, I drove with Jasmine on Monday. This was her first drive with me. She maneuvered the car pretty well. She seemed to lose focus and had a difficult time with left and right.

A couple of times I asked her to turn one way and she went the opposite.

At the end of one drive, we needed to make a left turn into the bus barn parking lot. We were traveling east on 11th St., in the right lane with a car on our left. Another vehicle was coming at us in the westbound lanes. Not wanting to try the impossible, I instructed Jasmine, "Turn right at the next street. We can go around the block and try again." Instead, she pulled to the left, somehow avoiding a sideswipe. Then she attempted to make the left turn. I hit my brake with full force then wrestled the wheel from her, avoiding a head-on collision.

I was afraid to take her to Davenport for our last drive so we went to Clinton for the second time. On the first Clinton trip we were working on left turns onto the one-way streets. I told her five times to always turn into the closest lane before she finally got it right. This trip she was actually doing better than usual, and I was considering not making her drive with the DOT. Then downtown she tried to turn left on a green light in front of oncoming traffic.

Jasmine drove a moped every day to and from school. You would think that would have helped, but it didn't. She also said she was being flipped off all the time while driving. No wonder. When I informed her Dad she was going to have to take the drive test, I wish I could remember his clever comment. He wasn't at all surprised — he had driven with her, too.

One Saturday six months later, I was teaching in DeWitt again. We changed drivers every two hours at the bus barn. Up drove Jasmine's father and he asked, "How does a student get a new certificate of completion if she lost the original?" When I saw Jasmine in the passenger seat, why was I not surprised?

A friend was working with a student who kept using her left foot on the brake. You're supposed to use your left foot only if you drive a standard shift vehicle. He had the girl take her left shoe off and it worked. This solved the problem of using her wrong foot. Contrary to popular belief, it is not illegal to drive barefoot. I normally wouldn't recommend it, however.

I drive with 130 students annually. About once or twice a year I get a student who has major processing challenges and is unable to comprehend two pieces of information or two directions at once, such as, "At the second stop sign, turn right." Yet we are supposed to help them become independent drivers.

Dance and athletics are great for developing coordination and processing skills. Generally, active teens learn to drive more quickly than sedentary teens. The thinking process and coordination skills improve with practice.

Good Communication

We worry about our children's safety on the road. Are they getting our message: "Be a responsible driver"? Here is a modified version of the quote we have all heard: "Mom, Dad, how you drive speaks so loudly, what you preach I cannot hear." Our children have spent thousands of hours observing the way we drive. They will obey or disobey the same traffic laws we do. For some of us, that is exciting. For others, it is discouraging. It may not be too late, however, to start setting a good example.

Kids don't always get the message right. There is a story told about an 8-year-old little girl. Her Mom was taking her to a friend's house to play. She asked, "Mommy, how old are you?" "That's kind of personal," her mother responded.

"Then tell me, how much do you weigh?" she asked. "That's even more personal!"

"Then tell me why did you and Daddy get a divorce."

"Okay, no more questions."

When she got to her friend's house, the friend said, "Just look at her license. Everything you ever wanted to know about your mother is there."

That night at home she said, "Mommy, I know you're 32 years old."

"That is amazing," Mom said.

"You weight 130 pounds," she said.

"How did you figure that out?" Mom asked.

"I also know why you and Daddy got a divorce."

"I am sure you do. Why did we get a divorce?" Mom asked.

"You got an F in sex."

Talking about taking instructions literally, Kevin was driving with a student on a hot day early in the school year. He asked this big, strong kid to "Crack the window." Back in the day, that meant to open the window a bit. The boy didn't understand, so with his powerful fist he literally cracked the passenger's side window.

On occasion, Audrey, Kevin and Will would practice driving with their special needs students. One day Kevin was driving with a boy using his personal car, a Ford Pinto. The Chevy Corvair was already taken off the market, so the only other cars on the road as dangerous were the Volkswagen Bug, the Vega, and the Chevette that had an optional back seat.

They drove east around a curve on old Highway 30. The boy didn't see the stop sign or get the teacher's instruction to brake. Picture a 6-foot, 5-inch-tall ex-football lineman sardined in this car as it is about to be run over by a semi traveling at 65 mph on the four-lane highway. The student's foot was covering the Pinto's brake, so the teacher with all his strength pushed the driver's leg to the floor to engage the brake, saving their lives. He looked like a ghost upon his return to school. This was the last day they ever practiced with their students.

I heard two more stories when I gave blood recently at the local high school blood drive. Jessica, 17, had a baby and decided to graduate early. She took driver's education so she could drive herself to work and be better able to care for her child. Mom and Dad bought her a Mustang for graduation and 18th birthday gift. To save money, she covered it with liability insurance only.

On her birthday, she was out celebrating with a friend when the friend, pointing out a hot guy, stuck her left arm in front of Jessica. This blocked her view and she rear-ended another car. The crash was her fault and the insurance didn't cover the damage to Jessica's car. She is still upset, 23 years later. I forgot to ask if she and her former passenger still speak to one another.

Hope is older and got her license in the winter of 1979. Because the snow was piled so high, all intersections were pretty much blind. She pulled forward to be able to see. The lady passing by went into an icy slide after hitting her brake too hard. This caused her to crash into Hope, who was then ticketed because she was the one at the stop sign. She, 36 years later, is still not happy that she got a ticket.

Students are required to have their permit with them any time they drive. Rebecca lost hers, she informed me during our 7 a.m. class. Fortunately, she had all day to get it replaced before our evening driving session.

She and a parent had to go 60 miles round-trip from Wheatland to Clinton to get a new permit. The trip took two hours, they burned two or three gallons of gas, and the replacement permit cost $10. That night I asked Rebecca, " How did it go?"

"My parents hollered at me for the first three hours," she admitted. "After that it wasn't too bad."

Let others know your intentions. This is what signals are for.

Too Close To The Curb

One September, I experienced 36 of the most stressful hours I have ever had in a driver's ed car. The parents of these six students never practiced driving with their children. The kids drove poorly in town, but it got worse when they started driving on the highway with no experience.

One of these six was Chandra, driving on a Friday night in the 5 to 7 p.m. session. She was nice but awfully nervous and very pregnant. She commented that she had never practiced parking, a skill we practice a lot on the first drive. She said she had done all of her driving on the street. After climbing behind the wheel, she asked, "Which foot pedal is the big one, the gas or the brake?" This was a tough drive, even though most of it was in a parking lot.

She was scheduled to drive again the next morning but was a no-show. Later, I learned she had delivered her baby on Saturday morning during her scheduled drive time.

Chandra came back to drive the following Friday. "I started having contractions in the early morning hours," she told me. "I went to the hospital at 6 a.m. and had a baby girl late that morning."

Again, she was very anxious on this second drive. We were heading west on River Drive with almost no traffic at 8:10 p.m. At 20 mph she attempted to turn right 20 feet before we reached the intersection at Brady Street, a one-way street going north. When we hit the curb, we flattened the front right tire and mashed the rim. Fortunately, I was able to maneuver the car around the corner and park under a streetlight where we changed the tire. It took only 15 minutes.

The next morning I called my boss, Autumn. She met us 45 minutes later and we switched out cars. It was best not to drive all day Saturday and Sunday on a donut-undersized spare tire. Autumn wasn't too concerned. "This stuff happens in driver education," she said.

Chandra never told her mother about the wheel. I guess this new Grandmother already had too much on her plate to burden her with a crash. Chandra will graduate early, in December, with plans to start working as a CNA. She knew she was going to need to drive if she was going to make it. Students are not allowed to drive unless they have their permit with them. On the next day, Saturday, Allie left her permit at home. Zooey also didn't have her permit, but she did find it when we stopped at her house. Then she tried to drive into the curb, cutting the turn too short just as Chandra had done the night before. This time I slammed on the brake, so we just bumped the curb.

For the rest of the fall classes, I was more nervous than usual. In September, with six novice drivers, we had had several close encounters with the curb and parked vehicles.

Allie and Joe were brother and sister. She was a senior with a little practice and he a junior who had never driven before. Allie never improved. Joe was an athlete, so his coordination helped him learn quickly. Often an athlete's biomechanics and cognitive skills are better and they learn much faster.

On the first drive Allie didn't have her permit; she thought she had lost it. The driving station was open on Saturday morning so she could get a new one for $10. Then she would have it for tomorrow's Sunday drive. She did find it and she saved the money. On our third drive she didn't have it again. With a call and a stop at her Dad's work, we got it out of his car.

If a student permit is stamped, the student must take the drive test with a DOT official at the driving station. I ended up stamping three and could have stamped all six in this September class. Normally I stamp fewer than 10% of my drive students.

In one school where I teach there is a rule. If you open a gate, you close it when you leave. If you unlock a room, lock it back up when you're done. If you turn on a light, turn it off when you're finished. If you don't open up, unlock, or turn off, leave it alone.

While teaching the May class, I unlocked the gate to go in and retrieve the driver education car from the shop. Apparently someone followed me in. When I left I didn't see anyone around, so I left, locking the gate behind me. The next morning, Saturday, the same car was parked in the same place. I hope that driver learned that you don't take your car in somewhere you don't belong, unless you plan on leaving your car over the weekend.

I wish parents would understand the danger they put their children in when they allow them to get a license without the needed practice. Most teen fatalities happen to these very kids. The State Farm Insurance website tells us that a driver is not considered experienced with fewer than 1,000 hours of practice.

Now more teens are waiting until they turn 18 to get a driver's license. Stupid! At least, this is my opinion. They are not that interested and don't want to invest the time, money and effort that is required to become a safe driver. They aren't taught and they don't have the driving experience. This is the reason deaths of 18- to 24-year-old drivers are on the rise. If you know a teen who is considering waiting to get a license, please persuade that teen to get the practice and proper training. In fact, encourage students to always drive when the family goes anywhere.

My insurance agent says Iowa has the second lowest automobile insurance rates in the nation. According to a friend, an Iowa State Trooper, the feds are trying to make Iowa raise its permit age of 14 to match that of other states.

Why would you want to mess with what is working? Maybe giving teens one or two years more practice is what is saving lives.

Have you heard the oxymoron? "I am from the federal government and I am here to help you."

Chapter 3: Define "Responsible"

Cell Phones

During a driving session with students, I saw a woman reading on her Kindle device while driving down the highway. We've had someone pull out in front of us on a bicycle while texting. My wife saw a man on a motorcycle pull away from a stoplight, texting as he drove through the intersection. Almost every time I'm out in the driver's ed car, I see someone texting.

Every time she sees someone driving and texting, my daughter's friend blasts her horn. I asked my trooper friend about it. He said he didn't think it would hurt anything.

I am contemplating making a sign that says "Texting Kills." Then whenever I pass a violator, I would honk and hold up the sign for the texter to read.

George told me about his neighbor girl who, while texting, drove off the gravel road into his cornfield at harvest time. He didn't have her charged, but she was required to pick all the corn she had mowed down. With the help of Mom and Dad and a sibling she completed the task. A great lesson, more valuable than a fine.

Jean, a friend and fellow teacher from years ago, told this story. About five years ago her granddaughter in New Jersey was taking driver education. There, all students take driver education through private schools. The young instructor told his students that it was okay to text. Just make sure you hold the phone down below the dash. The Mom called and reported the teacher. He is probably now in another line of work.

Brad and I swam at the Iowa Games one weekend. He showed me a photo. His friend who was a semi driver recently had a girl veer right under his truck. She was unhurt and fortunately had no passengers. The whole right side of her car was mangled. A rider would have died instantly.

When she realized what she had done the first words out of her mouth were, "Where is my phone?"

Years ago Brad lived in South Carolina. Not happy with the school his kids were in, he enrolled them in a Christian school. Soon after, he was driving down the highway, stuck behind a big truck with a tailgater on his rear. When Brad finally had a chance to pass, he was almost hit by the guy behind. His reaction was to flip him off. Then he noticed the crazy driver was his minister from church.

Later Brad apologized to the guy for his inappropriate gesture. Then he told the minister he was endangering others' lives, and wasn't going to be of much help to his congregation if he was dead. I hope this was a good lesson for all involved.

A friend shared they recently passed a guy on the highway who was using his cell phone, plus eating with chopsticks, apparently using his knees to steer with. He noted he was not Asian.

Julie, an eastern Iowa library director, shared this story. Last spring, she was on her way home driving on Spruce Hills Drive in Davenport. She was almost ready to move to the left-hand turning lane to turn onto East Kimberly Road. With rush hour, there was a lot of stop-and-go traffic, and she couldn't quite pull into the turning lane just yet. As she waited in the left lane, she looked up in the rearview mirror and saw a younger girl behind her who was clearly texting on her phone while at the wheel. She would look up and inch closer to Julie's car and then look back down to her lap. Julie had the sinking feeling: "She's going to hit my car."

Sure enough, the car in front of Julie started to go. Julie drove forward. The car behind her pulled forward just as the car in front of her stopped suddenly. Julie stopped, but the girl crashed into the back of her vehicle and pushed her car into the car in front of her. When Julie got out of the car to check the damage, the dumbfounded girl said, "You stopped so suddenly!" To which Julie replied, "Yes, because the car in front of me did."

The girl, a senior in high school, later sheepishly remarked that she had been in three prior accidents that year. I think I know why.

Two years ago, a former student was killed on Highway 61, just one-and-a-half miles from my home. The Welton gas station intersection is dangerous. This is an oblique angle intersection for those turning right from the west. When cars maneuver so Highway 61 is at 90 degrees, it is much easier and safer to see traffic coming from the north on their left.

That day, I was told, there was an initial crash caused by a person messing with a CD player. Naturally, traffic slowed. Because this young lady approaching the intersection was typing on her phone, she didn't see the half-mile traffic back-up. The instant she posted her message on Facebook she rear-ended a semi and died. Tragically, a 4-year-old little boy was left an orphan.

Below is a letter I sent to our state legislators about taking serious action this session to help eliminate driving and texting:

January 26, 2015

Dear Iowa Legislators,

It took Candy Lightner and her organization MADD to get Americans to seriously consider removing drunk drivers from our highways. Today, our alcohol-related fatalities are down from nearly 60% in 1990 to 32%. With increased miles driven today figured in, our alcohol fatality rate is only half of what it was 25 years ago. She succeeded in a big way.

With the removal of drunks, and with better roads, improved vehicles and education, yearly national highway fatalities have come down to 36,000, the lowest in decades, until recently. Now because of texting, highway deaths are starting to climb back up.

Texting while driving is several times more dangerous than drunk driving. During a five-second look-away, a car travels more than the length of a football field. Why are we not working to stop this threat on our highways?

Our lawmakers have made texting a secondary offense. This is a useless law. Drivers cannot be pulled over while texting. Their behavior is not going to change until legislators fix this problem by making texting a primary offense. Let law enforcement make our highways safer with laws they can actually enforce.

Iowa seatbelt fines are high: $195.50 for drivers under 18 and $127.50 for adult drivers. I believe this is why compliance is around 95%.

Let's make texting a primary offense with stiff fines. When government wants to stop a behavior they tax the heck out of it. If we want to get serious about stopping this epidemic, hit people's pocketbooks hard.

We could also make backseat seatbelt use mandatory. This would save even more lives.

—Bill Mueller

Texting is now illegal for all drivers in Iowa. In the United States, almost 25 percent of all crashes are caused by drivers using their phone. You are 23 times more likely to crash while texting. Six times more crashes are caused by people texting than by drunk drivers.[9] At 55 mph you travel over 100 yards each time you look from the roadway for five seconds. It is like having a blindfold on.

People complain about teenagers, but almost all the drivers I see texting are adults. You know before you ever pass them. Texters used to go slower than the flow of traffic. They were all over the highway. When you went around them they were looking at their lap or down at the steering wheel.

What is so important that you can't wait until you arrive safely? Today you see people texting making all the same mistakes, but now they are often passing you.

We all need to witness the interview on a video clip with the all-important person on the other end of the line, after their friend, sister, daughter, or son just died as a result of texting on the road. It will tear your heart out.

Frequently I ask students why they need their phones on while driving. They say, "There might be an emergency." Then I ask, "How many of you in the past month have had a true emergency while in a car?"

The answer is always zero.

Don't Mess With Me

If anyone ever messes with a driver education car, we call 911. Teenagers are sometimes tempted to mess with their friends while driving. Most realize the resulting fine wouldn't be worth it.

Once driving down Highway 136 we were "mooned." I was so surprised that we didn't get the license number or a picture for evidence. That would have cost the people mooning us big bucks.

Another time we were turning left into the Clinton High School parking lot. We had to wait for the traffic to pass. As we were making our turn, a rough-looking guy 50 or 55 years of age, in a beat up old minivan, tried to pass in the far left lane.

He almost hit us. He was enraged because he thought we pulled out in front of him. This doesn't make any sense because you don't turn into a parking lot from a parking space along the curb.

This guy followed us to the back of the school, and proceeded to disrespectfully vent at the student driver and me. After unsuccessfully trying to reason with him, finally I said, "Sir, if you continue to harass us you will be explaining this to the police." I wrote down his license number. He got the message, got in his wreck and unhappily departed.

Night Driving and Fatigue

About 25 years ago I was pulled over by an Illinois State Trooper for drifting in my lane. It was late on a weeknight and he knew I wasn't drinking. I had Iowa plates and was driving on the interstate. We were about a mile from the next tollbooth so he suggested I pull over there. I got some sleep and when rested continued my trip home.

After that wake-up call I have stopped a hundred times. Only once did I have a deputy stop to see if I was okay while sleeping under a parking lot security light. Law enforcement knows you're resting and prefers that you stay off the road until you are ready to safely continue your drive.

Audrey's and my families live in Wisconsin. When our children were little we often departed at 8 or 10 pm. With little kids, it was always easier if they slept in the car. Our parents never understood the logic, but they were always happy to see the grandkids.

We used to argue about stopping. Audrey had trouble staying alert herself but was afraid we were going to get mugged if we stopped and slept. I decided long ago we were not going to be a statistic because I couldn't stay awake. Now whenever she notices me rubbing the back of my neck, a sign I am tired, we pull off the highway. I prefer my odds comfortably sleeping in a lit rest area.

Our son and his family live 1,100 miles away near Austin, Texas. Audrey and I visit three times a year, always anxious to see Tyler, Sam, and our grandkids Isabella and Tristan. Because I hate wasting two extra days on the road each trip, we always drive straight through and almost always at night. After dark, you never have to deal with the rush hours of Kansas City, Oklahoma City, or Dallas. Also, there aren't too many crashes that close down the freeway.

I always get some rest before we leave. On our drive, we listen to audio books, which make the trip seem about half as far. The library has hundreds of titles. If I get tired, we stop and take a nap in Kansas or Oklahoma. Coming home, if I pull over to sleep it is usually in southern Iowa.

A friend often used to travel home late at night. Once about 25 years ago the rest area 30 miles from home looked pretty inviting. He was exhausted and just had to stop. He pulled up next to the lone trash barrel and picnic table and nodded off. After a few minutes of sleep, he drove home alert.

He later learned that a young woman's body was found in the barrel the very next day. That experience really shook him. He never again stopped short of home unless he was checking into a hotel. Six or seven years ago, almost 20 years later, using DNA, authorities apprehended the person who killed the girl. The murderer is in prison for many years to come.

We were driving to our daughter's in Mt. Vernon one Friday night last August along Highway 30 between Lowden and Clarence. Ahead, I spotted a white SUV swerving into the lane of an oncoming semi. At the last moment, the vehicle jerked back into our lane. Soon it pulled over on the shoulder.

Worried there was an emergency, Audrey convinced me to go back to make sure everything was okay. A woman had fallen asleep behind the wheel after working several 10-hour shifts that week. She appreciated our stopping. Though shaking from her near-death experience, she was close to home and could make it safely.

One in every six deadly car crashes results from a fatigue-impaired driver, estimates the National Highway Traffic Safety Administration. That's compared to about one in three caused by a drunk driver. [10]

Fatigue impairs ability to perform even basic driving tasks. Fatigue decreases reaction time, affects judgment, and can cause erratic driving behavior. Even though there may be some sleepy drivers on the road, if the weather is good and you are alert, I believe travel by night on the expressway is safer than day travel.

There is less traffic. Rush hour and its associated crashes are never a concern. Why is it called "rush hour" when you hardly move anywhere? Nocturnal travel also eliminates major stress for the nervous city driver, unless suffering from night blindness.

Visibility is better when using your bright lights. If others are near you, drive with your dims because then you can see potential hazards with the lights of other travelers. If there are intoxicated, fatigued, or distracted drivers going in your direction, they are easier to spot. You can call 911 to get them off the road.

Traveling at night, it is best to have a co-pilot stay awake with the driver to help navigate and monitor the driver's alertness. When you have multiple drivers you can tag-team your drive. If you get tired, stop for coffee or something cold to drink. Eat a snack or chew on ice. Get out and stretch. If these techniques don't help, pull into a well-lit rest area or a store parking lot and get some sleep.

Respect

Amanda was a tiny girl under five feet tall and a very good student driver. On her first drive ever, she was with her Dad on 53rd Avenue in Bettendorf, the busiest street in the Quad Cities. Someone flipped her off. What a confidence builder.

Three years ago we were at Casey's convenience store in Key West, south of Dubuque. It is an always-crowded parking lot. A man and woman in their 20s almost collided while both were backing up. The lady was at fault as much as the man.

Within 10 feet of him, she flipped him off. How could she have such a low opinion of herself and others that she could humiliate another person in that manner? What if he had pulled her out of her car and pummeled her?

One summer, we had our driver education car egged the night after our second class. The school's superintendent said, "That's funny, none of our other cars got vandalized." Later I learned from my students that this was a common occurrence in this small town. I guess there is a real shortage of other entertainment available.

I heard on the radio a couple of summers ago a guy in Austin, Texas, got mad at another driver. At the next red light, he shot out his back window. I would be curious to know what the other driver had done to cause that kind of anger.

My old neighbor Roy hates mufflers, seatbelts, and bicyclists. His lawn service and cattle enterprises require him to frequently pull a trailer with either equipment or livestock on the highway. He gets very frustrated with bicyclists and their antics.

I have cycled thousands of miles myself and have witnessed how many riders don't obey the traffic laws and make travel for cars and trucks more difficult.

About five years ago, Roy and I were sitting in my hot tub where we argue politics, religion, lawyers, and the long arm of the law. Roy shared the events of the last couple of days.

The day before, he was traveling south of town on Old Highway 61. Pulling his lawn equipment trailer, he nudged a couple of bicyclists onto the shoulder of the road. After passing, he flipped them off.

The very next day he was pulled over by Randy, the sheriff, a friend from church, whose kids attended school with our kids. Randy wrote him up for three violations: no seatbelt (back then it was only $85, now it is $127.50), no muffler, and the third for a bad trailer light. The total was about $200.

After giving Roy the paperwork for the tickets, the sheriff said, "Do you remember yesterday traveling down this highway when you ran a man and a woman on their bikes off the road?"

Roy thought for a moment and said, "I think so." The sheriff said, "Then do you remember after endangering their lives you passed and flipped them off?" Roy again reflected for a bit and said, "I think so."

The sheriff said, "That was my wife and I."

Roy told me the story that evening and admitted that he had it coming. A few months later I ran into Randy, the sheriff, and he told me his version. Being a bicycle enthusiast, his slant was different, but enjoyable, nonetheless.

Never flip anyone off; you never know how it may come back to bite you.

I give various talks to area teen, parent, civic or senior groups.

My goal is to help make our streets and highways safer by presenting a common-sense look at many of the frequent and challenging aspects of driving, and sharing funny stories I have gained from personal experience or gleaned from others' driving experiences.

I spoke to the Lions' Club about four years ago, concluding with the story of Roy and Randy accompanied with much laughter. When I finished, Stella, a sweet 80-something senior, came up afterward and said, "I loved your talk; it was so educational and funny. It was the best we have had in ages."

Then she said. "I do have one question, what does it mean to flip someone off?" I told her, "It was when you give someone the finger." If she still didn't know, I'm pretty certain her husband could tell her.

I knew a guy who had both road rage and a monster pickup. In a traffic jam someone cut him off, so he drove up on top of their car.

One time, my brother and his friends attended a school dance. The guys without dates soon were bored. They borrowed my brother's car. These guys drove around Racine mooning unsuspecting victims, each time speeding away, enjoying the joke. This worked pretty well until they mooned a couple. The man chased them on foot to no avail, but he was able to identify the vehicle and its 80-pound mooner.

The police apprehended the pranksters and the red car with the white trunk when they returned to the dance as it was all over. One of them was Lonny, the 80-pound senior the size of a 12-year-old.

My brother and his date hopped in and accompanied their friends to the police station. Because they weren't involved, they were allowed to leave.

Each perpetrator had to call home for a ride. The resulting calls were unpleasant for everyone involved. At midnight an anxious Lonny, the mooner, woke his Dad, not a very nice man even in the daytime. "Who is this?" Dad growled.

"Dad it's me," Lonny said.

"What do you want?" Dad barked.

"Dad, I'm in jail."

"What for?"

"I was caught mooning."

Dad bellowed, "What's that?"

Nervously Lonny said, "Well, that is when you pull your pants down and stick your bare rear end out the window."

Dad thought for a moment, then screamed, "When your case comes to court, plead insanity," and slammed down the phone.

One day we were driving over by the Iowa Machine Shed Restaurant in West Davenport. There are two lanes in each direction. We were in the left lane and a red pickup was next to us in the right. A little green car pulled out right in front of him and he immediately hit his brake and turned. The truck driver swerved, almost hitting us, and flipped off the driver of the other car.

How ironic. It was okay for the driver of the pickup to cut us off, giving the finger to the other person who did the very same thing to him.

Peter's Dad, a urologist from Bettendorf, told of their San Francisco trip 18 years ago. His wife and he, newly married, were visiting her brother in California.

They were traveling in lane six of an eight-lane highway. Realizing they had to exit right they started their track in that direction at 60 mph. Pulling into lane five, they didn't realize the car approaching was cruising at 80 mph.

In a rage, the guy went around them, slowing before pitching a milkshake onto their windshield, blinding Dr. Hanson and putting lives in danger.

I wonder what the fine for attempted murder is?

My sister Jane lives in Bristol, Wis. One of her daughters lives in a Chicago suburb near O'Hare Airport. Recently Jane was in Chicago and lost her way.

As she picked up her GPS, a policeman spotted her and thought she was on her cell phone. She was fined $120 for using a phone in Chicago while driving. Jane admits she was not too polite to the policeman because she had not been breaking the law.

Jane decided to fight it in court. She arrived with her phone records in hand to prove that she was innocent of the charge. When she went before the judge, he was rude and disrespectful.

He thought she was nuts for challenging the system. Even if she was found innocent, her court costs were going to be $194.

To me it seems that the legal system of Chicago is in the business of extortion. Even if you are innocent, you are forced to pay the ticket because it is cheaper than going to court. Where is the justice in that?

After listening to Jane's story, the judge told her she should go sit down and decide what she wanted to do. Upon returning before him, she explained that a person should not be forced to pay any amount of money if there was evidence that she had not committed a crime. He could not believe that a person would actually take a day off work and travel from Wisconsin to Chicago to fight a ticket.

Though he was in an irritated state, Jane must have touched his heart. He told her that if she promised to leave his court and never come back, he would drop all charges and fines against her.

Two ladies had been sitting next to her. One was bawling probably because she saw how belligerent the judge was to an innocent person.

The second was astounded; this was the first time she had ever seen anyone escape this courtroom without having to pay. Jane took the $120 and gave it to her favorite charity. They were sure to use it more wisely than Chicago's justice system.

This reminds me of the bully who is taking kids' lunch money. "If you are going to use this sidewalk on your way to school we are going to force you to pay a sidewalk tax."

With this extortion being the standard practice in Chicago, how is it any different from greasing the palms of officials if you want to travel in some Third-World countries.

Speed

My friend Merlyn was once driving in Los Angeles traveling 10 miles per hour faster than the posted speed limit in the right lane so he wouldn't get run over. A policeman pulled alongside and motioned for him to speed up. He was holding up traffic and was a hazard in this situation where everyone was traveling at the higher common speed.

Red, my college roommate of three years, was pulled over for speeding while making a run for hamburgers and French fries. When the cop reached the car, he was surprised to see it full of college guys all wearing Burger King cardboard crowns.

No one in the car looked mature enough to be driving. I don't remember if he was cited or not.

A friend, Michael, drives faster than he should. He is a devout Christian and wants to put a symbol of a fish on his car.

Brianne, his wife, won't let him. She says he's a bad witness.

I had my children, Whitney, Tyler and Marcy, all driving big cars while they were in high school. I thought this would give them more protection. I learned from Lance, an auxiliary policeman, 10 years after Ty's graduation, that they clocked him in our Crown Victoria at 106 mph.

They weren't sure of his actual speed, because when they spotted him the front end of the car was pointing down in an attempt to stop. In retrospect this would have been a safer car only if it had a four-cylinder engine.

Have you ever known any slow learners? This story was aired on a Kenosha radio station December 26, 2014. On December 13, a Chicago man, age 24, was picked up twice in 15 minutes on Interstate 94 while driving to work.

At 7:27 a.m. he was stopped at Highway KR, the Kenosha-Racine County Line Road. He was going 90 mph in a 65 mph zone. It cost $301.30 and six points off his license.

The second speeding violation was at Highway C at 7:42 a.m. This time he was traveling 85 mph. It cost him $276.10 and six more points off his license. Plus, in Wisconsin, 25 miles per hour over the speed limit is an automatic license revocation for 15 days. I bet he was fun to work with that day. He would have saved a ton of money and heartache if he had just slept in.

I was speaking to a local civic group one Tuesday. These were some stories that the guests told.

Joe, 15 years ago, was picked up three blocks from his home for an OWI, Operating While Intoxicated. He hasn't had a drink since. His son has been picked up three times for the same offense. Joe doesn't like the long arm of the law.

Joe enjoyed sharing the following: "Today on the right shoulder at the south end of town was sitting a police car with its lights flashing. One of the town's residents drove by and was unable to move over because the left lane was already occupied. She did slow as she passed the policeman. The officer engaged his siren, pulled her over, and ticketed her for violating the move-over law."

Everyone at this gathering was speculating whether she would have to pay the $295 fine. If the information I was given is correct, the cop is wrong. He will probably get a chewing out for ticketing a woman who had not violated the law and was married to a local lawyer.

In 1901, what do you think would have been considered a safe speed to travel? That year Connecticut passed the nation's first speed laws. They decided anything over 12 mph in the city, and 15 mph in the country was excessive and just too dangerous. Drivers were also required to slow for horse-drawn vehicles.

In 1930 there were still a dozen states with no speed laws. [11]

Highways are posted with maximum speed signs. This is the speed under ideal conditions. The basic speed is speed that is safe for the current conditions. Common speed is the speed that most people are driving on the expressway.

Travel

My senior year in high school I visited UW-Milwaukee, UW-La Crosse, UW-Parkside, Marquette University, and Saint Norbert College.

I then went to visit Loras College on the recommendation of Jim Welsh, my high school wrestling coach. He had a friend who was an alumnus. I wanted to wrestle, and at the time Iowa wrestling was king.

I was a farm boy from a big family of 11 kids, and had no dependable transportation. My buddy, Doc, and I decided to hitchhike to Dubuque for my college visit. We left from Kenosha, Wis., one Friday morning in April. We arrived at Loras about noon, and returned on Saturday afternoon because Doc had to work the night shift at the Racine Journal Newspaper.

Pat Flanagan, Loras wrestling coach, introduced me to the most dedicated, sharing college staff anywhere. The financial aid director, Charlie McCormick, worked very hard on the money details so I could become part of the Loras family. I wouldn't trade my college experience for anything and I still think Loras is the prettiest campus in America.

I hitched home to Kenosha on my first Labor Day weekend. At that point I hadn't had much experience traveling with my thumb. I soon had my doubts as to whether this method of travel was such a good idea. The very first person to pick me up was a guy looking for action. After I turned him down, he quickly dropped me off about five miles from Dubuque. I had 155 miles to go, and there really was no going back.

I hitched a lot to Platteville, about 25 miles away. My brother Mark was a freshman at UW Platteville while I was a freshman at Loras College. If I could make it there, I usually could get a lift home to Kenosha, or back to Dubuque. That is, as long as I was willing to chip in for gas. I don't recommend hitchhiking these days; it's dangerous, and now it's against the law.

I always wore a white T-shirt and carried a sign that said "Student" to and from my destination. Most of the people I hitched rides with worked in Dubuque. Some of these guys drove so fast, sometimes I got back to school faster than if I had had my own car.

A guy in a VW Beetle once picked me up. He had a Saint Bernard that filled the whole back seat. It was a friendly giant that hadn't bathed in weeks and drooled all over me.

My sophomore year, my sister Jane and Audrey, now my wife of 39 years, were freshmen at Platteville. Jane was given an old black Rambler sedan after graduation. It came from Anita and Ollie. It had been used for deliveries to and from the restaurant they owned, which was next to our farm. They were also one of my Mom's milk customers. The car still had a slight sour milk smell.

I never had my own car until my senior year. Then I needed one to student teach. My sophomore and junior years I usually had use of Jane's car when I got to Platteville. In warm weather I could ride the 350 Honda that Mark and I owned together.

Tony, a good friend, was a student in meteorology and computer science at UW-Madison. I used to hitch to the Badger football games. I saw five in all.

Audrey even hitched with me to one game. This was during Wisconsin's only two successful football seasons before Coach Barry Alvarez came to town and changed the culture into a winning football program.

At Wisconsin's Camp Randall stadium, alcohol was prohibited. Most students carried in flasks with unidentified beverages anyway. Half the students who left the stadium were so impaired they didn't know who had won or lost.

During my sophomore or junior year, I started catching a ride back to Dubuque on Monday mornings with a professor. He was a wonderful man, the band director at our college.

One Saturday my junior year we won the Maranantha Bible College wrestling tournament in Watertown, Wis. That night on our way back to Dubuque, Iowa, I was dropped off at Platteville so I could see Audrey and celebrate.

We had a blizzard the next day. Coach wasn't too pleased with me when I couldn't get back to wrestling practice on Monday. We were preparing for our district meet that next weekend.

In four years that was the only practice I ever missed except for once when I was studying for a test.

I did get my own car senior year, an American Motor's Gremlin; American Motors bought out Rambler Corporation. It may have been safer hitchhiking than driving that car.

Matt tells about one of their Boy Scout trips. Their leader was chauffeuring a Suburban full of boys, pulling a trailer with the troop's equipment up the Andalusia Hill in Illinois. The truck's back left axle exploded, rocketing the wheel at the motorcyclist following.

In his mirror, the driver saw the spinning disk almost take the biker's head off. The four-wheeled trailer kept the back of the truck off the ground.

He was able to stop quickly with no injuries and no further damage. It did give everyone quite a scare and unfortunately cost $1,600 to repair.

We were traveling through Missouri last July. We got our van soaked by a crop-spraying airplane.

Chapter 4: Maintenance, Mirrors, and More

Keys

Jim ate lunch with his granddaughter at Burger King. When they left the restaurant, Katie's fob wouldn't open her car door. This was puzzling and had never happened before. She had no idea what to do.

Grandpa asked for her keys. Inserting the key in the door, he proceeded to open her door. Dumbfounded, she had never seen a key used in such a manner.

Oh, have times changed in this high-tech world.

I was told that years ago car companies had only five different keys for all of their vehicles. One night after a function, Mom got in her station wagon to go home. Ramblers were made in Kenosha, and half the cars on the road were that make.

To her shock, the radio blasted to attention when she turned on the ignition. Back then the radio was an option she didn't have in her vehicle. She was in the wrong car.

Carburetors

Remember back when cars were bigger, heavier, and more temperamental? Carburetors fueled the engine back before fuel injection was invented. Both manual transmission clutch cars and automatics were challenging. Many families had at least one vehicle—car, truck or tractor—that didn't function at peak performance.

If you are over age 50 you probably remember using both feet to keep your car running. Today using two feet to operate an automatic is considered a mortal sin.

In cold weather, engines were especially difficult. People would spray ether in the carburetor to get them to run. One sub-zero night, over Dad's objections, Mom took us to see the new release "One Hundred and One Dalmatians." When the movie was over, Dad had to come to our rescue and get the car started.

On many frigid occasions, I held the light in our old horse barn while Dad cursed his International H tractor for not starting. Fifty years later we still use that warm weather tractor for all the hayrides at our family picnics.

Roger, a friend, was telling of his driver education experience in the late '60s. He grew up a farm boy in rural western Iowa. They came to a stop sign at a T intersection on a hill. The driver education car was a newer car in pretty good condition. His teacher told him to really give it the gas. The phrase "really give it the gas" can be a relative phrase.

To Roger, give it the gas meant keeping the car running. Really giving it the gas was what was required just to get their car to move.

With his teacher's insistence, Roger floored the car. They jumped through the T intersection. When the dust settled, the teacher realized they had landed in a farmer's field. He was beside himself. Roger said, "Oh, don't worry, these are my uncle's soybeans."

Maintenance

Phil, a fellow instructor, likes to tinker with his cars. He does all the simple maintenance. If you're like him and that is your interest, great. If not, have a professional do the necessary checks to help keep you safe while driving.

I have used synthetic oil for 25 years. All of my vehicles have gone more than 200,000 miles. Back in the 1960s, if a car reached 100,000 miles you celebrated a miracle. You might consider using this oil to lengthen the life of your automobile engine.

At a young age, I learned I had no interest in anything mechanical. Our first hay baler was a Roanoke. It was a big heavy monstrosity with 50 grease fittings. All were impossible to get to, I thought. My brother Mark, who was a year younger, loved working on this baler. I would have preferred walking five miles to school barefoot in January.

We drove a 1956 Chevy Bel Air to school. Dad bought it from a friend in 1971 for $100. The rust holes were filled with putty. The color was calico: white, turquoise and primer brown. The engine had a neat click when it ran. After graduation, my sister drove it. While she was coming home from school one day, the front wheel came off and continued rolling down the street.

She was so embarrassed she left the car and caught a ride home with a friend.

A trooper friend said that if we kept scrap cars off the road, we would eliminate the majority of the stalls along the highway. He is amazed at the reception he gets from passengers as he approaches the piece of junk they are driving. They are always surprised they broke down.

He is thinking, How did they ever make it this far?

In college, our daughter Marcy never noticed much when it came to the car she drove. By the time she brought a car noise to my attention, it always seemed to cost several hundred dollars.

My wife, Audrey, is just the opposite. She thinks she hears noises or feels vibrations before they actually occur. I'm always relieved when those concerns don't cost us much. Checking your vehicle on a regular schedule will save you in the long term.

My one brother and friends, Butch and Pat, took a dip in the creek. Dad gave Butch permission to drive his black-and-white beast of a car around the outside of our hay field.

None of the three friends were yet 16. Earlier Butch had problems with his brake line, but back then, parts stores weren't open on Sunday, so he just taped up the leak.

As they drove west toward the creek, Butch realized too late he had no brakes. Approaching the creek too fast, he panicked and overcorrected. This put the vehicle into a roll. They landed upside down in 12 inches of water. Back then there were no seat belts. Fortunately, they weren't thrown from the car, and the creek in the summer was low. The windows were open; they all escaped unharmed but soaked.

Early cars required frequent repairs. By 1920, machinists, blacksmiths, bicycle mechanics, and people with farm experience became the owners of 60,000 automobile repair shops. Between 1908-1927, Ford sold 15 million cars. Many of those years, Ford Motor Company sold over half the cars on the road.

Everyone learned to change and repair tires, which went flat frequently. Millions of owners loved their Fords, because they were easy to fix. Twine, baling wire, and clothespins were used to make minor repairs. This was before duct tape! The only tools needed were a screwdriver, wrench, hammer and pliers. With on-board computers today, shade-tree mechanics are long gone.[12]

In 1934, only seven years after Ford produced its last Model-T, the notorious Bonnie and Clyde were shot to death on May 23 in a stolen Ford automobile.[13]

According to AAA, crashes are the No. 1 reason for roadside assistance. Next is low battery; normally they should last 3-5 years. Lockouts are third. Bring a second set of keys when traveling. Fourth is transmission trouble. Fifth are brake problems. The final two are flat tires and running out of gas.

One of the main responsibilities of your vehicle ownership is to have it serviced regularly. Mechanics at certified shops will check fluids, hoses, tires, and parts to make sure everything is safe for the road.

Pay attention to the way your car handles, to noises, smells and lights on the instrument panel. If the light is yellow, have it checked by a professional. When the light is blinking yellow, it should be serviced promptly. Red means shut your vehicle off immediately and call for service.

Automobile Mirrors

Larry, a friend from bicycle spin class, remembers almost 50 years later a couple of harrowing episodes from his driver education days in western Iowa, where he grew up.

To celebrate the last drive, they went to Omaha and stopped for ice cream shakes. This was in the mid-'60s, when cars must not have had right side view mirrors, and air conditioning was rare.

To cool off, the boy in the right back seat had his window open with his plastic spoon sticking out catching the wind. The driver crossed a bridge so close to the rail that it knocked the spoon from the boy's hand.

He also shared the story of the girl a couple of years ahead of him. She was told to turn the left signal on for a turn. The shifter was on the column and she put the car in reverse, dropping the transmission in the middle of the street.

Rearview mirrors are used to see out the back window. A safe driver always knows what is going on around him or her. Side view mirrors are sometimes called door mirrors or wing mirrors, named after the wing windows that were in the early cars. These are used to help eliminate the blind spot on the rear quarters of the car. Some people also use an additional convex mirror for this purpose. Look in your mirrors at least every eight seconds.

For decades, drivers have been taught to adjust side view or wing mirrors to show the slightest amount of the side of the car. This is *incorrect*. This creates a triangular blind spot on each side of the car from the back seat and beyond.

Setting the left wing mirror, the driver should place his or her head a couple of inches from the driver's door window. When you can just see the side of the car in the mirror, this is the correct position. You set the right wing mirror by placing your head in front of the rearview mirror. Make sure you can now see the side of the car in the right wing mirror.

If the mirrors are adjusted properly you will eliminate all blind spots. Even if your mirrors are properly set as I've just advised, you should always make shoulder checks when backing, pulling out, or changing lanes.

Use of a mirror was first mentioned in "The Woman and The Car" in 1906. The first mounted mirror was used in 1911 at the inaugural "Indianapolis 500" race. Manufacturers first introduced the mirror in 1914.[14]

What a simple safety feature yet so important.

Safety Belts and Airbags

Rick was a senior in the mid-'60s. He tells of his experience with his wrestling and golf coach. This teacher was also his former driver education instructor. The team was returning from a golf meet in Anamosa in the driver education car.

Coach drove and Rick was the front seat passenger. For some unknown reason, Coach removed his seatbelt sometime during the trip and rebuckled it. Not even he noticed that he had reattached his seatbelt through the steering wheel.

Upon their return to Maquoketa, Coach attempted to make a right turn onto Summit Street by the golf course. The wheel wouldn't budge. As they forebodingly neared the ditch, Rick just instinctively stomped on the imaginary brake, the same reaction parents frequently have while teaching their children to drive. The car came to a screeching halt. They were saved by the dual brake, which comes standard in all driver education cars.

You have heard the expression, "You can't teach an old dog new tricks." Older people's brains are fully developed and it is more difficult for them to process new knowledge or technologies into their lives. May I change the saying to, "Some old dogs choose not to learn new tricks." Let me explain.

Roy was my neighbor for 15 years. He is a horse-trader who will sell anything for a price. Roy is a hard worker who adores kids. If he likes you, he loves you; if he doesn't, he will get even.

Earlier I shared that Roy hates mufflers, seatbelts, and bicyclists. You can always hear his pickup arriving or leaving. He owns a lawn service, 50 stock cows, and a prize bull, from which he sells 50 fat, feeder calves each year.

Roy is pushing 70 years of age and is stubborn. He has been ticketed at least a dozen times for not wearing a seatbelt. While sitting in my hot tub visiting last April, he explained he had already been picked up four times this year. He believes that all active safety devices like seatbelts are a nuisance.

I sometimes borrow Roy's pickup. His truck is a mess with its dents and half an exhaust system. Why would you ever spend money on an option like that? It has been driven hard and never cleaned. Audrey refuses to ride in it.

Last summer I needed to pick something up and he also had an errand to run. He graciously offered me a ride. With his cattle trailer attached. He speeds, rolls through stop signs, drives on the white fog line next to the shoulder, doesn't signal or notice other drivers. Riding with Roy going unsecured is a scary event. Have you ever dug through a bachelor's farm truck looking for a seat belt that has never been used?

I think subconsciously he wants to kick the bucket while driving his old high mileage pickup. I just hope that when his time comes, he doesn't take anyone with him.

My first car was a 1972 AMC six-cylinder standard transmission Gremlin in robin's egg blue turquoise. It looked as though the back half had been chopped off.

This was the car of my dreams. For $1,100, I purchased it in 1975, with 50,000 miles on it. I knew wearing my seat belt would be my only chance to survive a crash. This was the summer before my senior year of college. I needed a car so I could do my student teaching.

Do you remember in the 1970s when a car's life expectancy was 100,000 miles? Seat belts were optional, but I always wore mine. I feared getting rear-ended in my 1972 AMC Gremlin with no backend. Today it would be like getting rear-ended driving a Smart Car, one of those with no crush-zone protection.

I finally convinced Audrey to learn to drive this car, a clutch, during the 1977-78 school year in the mountains, actually the bluffs, of Dubuque, Iowa.

We drove this car to 125,000 miles. In 1980, our mechanic finally convinced me to unload it. By then the transmission had its own shift pattern. Audrey and I were the only people who knew the combination. Each time we had the oil changed, the techs at the shop got the shifter stuck. They convinced me that this vehicle was a death trap. Sadly, I parted with my first set of wheels. Actually, I was too tight to buy a newer, safer, more dependable car at the beginning of our married life.

Don tells about taking driver education in 1970. His teacher told the students to put on their safety belt. Back then there were only lap belts, and they weren't yet required by law. Don had never worn a seat belt or even seen one in use. He waited for the other two students to buckle up, so he could see how they were operated.

Recently, Don asked a student to roll down his window. Confused, the student asked, "How do you do that?" How times have changed since you don't roll down windows anymore. It is all push buttons.

Back before seat belts, one Halloween night a family friend was giving several of us a ride to trick or treat at some of our country neighbors' homes. The car door opened and my sister, 5-year-old Jane, fell out. Fortunately, we hadn't gone too far when Mrs. Jones was notified she had lost a passenger. When we went back to pick up Jane, we found her unhurt but less enthusiastic about this most popular of holidays.

73

My Mom had 13 siblings, seven of them girls. Throughout the 1930s my Grandfather was the softball coach. In one car he would load up the whole team and transport them to their various games around southeastern Wisconsin. Once a door came open while they were traveling down the highway. One player unfortunately mentioned this to her mother, and she was never again allowed to ride with the rest of the team. From that day forward, her Mom took her to every out-of-town game.

Drive-in theaters were popular when we were growing up. There were three within five miles of our farm. It was reasonable entertainment; I think we paid admission by the carload. Whenever Mom took us on outings, the Rambler station wagon was always full. No seat belts back then.

I have 10 siblings, no twins. At one point there were at seven of us under the age of eight. Most of our outings included seven of us plus a straggler friend or two who would join in. At the drive-in we fought over the front seat, because we could see the movie better.

On a nice night we could lie up on top of the car on a blanket, but then we couldn't hear the sound that came from the speaker on a cord which was attached to your window on the inside of the car.

Remember when an FM radio and air conditioning were options on a car? That was all we needed to be happy.

Seventy-five percent of all vehicle occupants who are totally ejected from the vehicle are killed. You are 25 times more likely to die if ejected from your vehicle than if you are wearing your seat belt.[15]

The first U.S. automobile seat belt patent was issued in 1885. This 2-Point seat belt was also called a lap belt. The child car seat was invented in 1921. It was basically a sack with a drawstring attached to the back seat. Volvo in 1939 introduced the 3-Point Child Seat. They also in 1959 brought to the market the modern lap/shoulder belt sometimes referred to as the combination belt.[16]

All states require passengers to use safety belts; most people refer to them as seat belts—any equipment you must engage in an active restraint device. Some states' requirements are stricter than those of other states.

Today, safety belts are designed to save lives, in conjunction with airbags. If the belts are not worn or are worn improperly, serious injury or even death can occur.

Airbags are a type of safety restraint. They are a passive restraint that works to protect the car's occupants without their having to engage the device. These are built into the steering wheel, dashboard, doors, roof or seats. They use a crash sensor to inflate, protecting the passenger from the impact of the crash.

Allen Breed invented the "sensor and safety system" in 1968. Twenty years later Chrysler finally offered airbags as standard equipment. They have been mandated in all cars since 1998.[17]

The Iowa seatbelt violation for adults in Iowa is $127.50. For teens under age 18 it costs almost $200. Our state's seat belt compliance is over 93%.[18] Most people here realize it is much easier to "click it" than to pay the fine.

Our state has one of the lowest rates of highway fatalities per capita in the nation. That is why our automobile insurance rates are among the lowest in the United States. Automobiles are engineered to protect their riders when they are properly seat-belted. Any time the passenger compartment is still intact following a crash, there should be no deaths. Many more lives would be saved if all passengers used seat belts every time they got in to a car.

People each year are killed by friends or loved ones who weren't wearing their belts. Many crash fatalities happen at 30-35 mph. The person unsecured flies through the vehicle like a pingpong ball. Weight x Speed = Force. For example, in a crash at 35 mph, a person weighing 200 pounds will kill other passengers with 7,000 pounds of force.

Wear your seatbelts.

Steering Wheel

Chuck taught driver's education for more than 30 years. I ran into him at the local bowling alley after he had a couple of adult beverages. We were discussing students who didn't understand steering. He said, "By the time they are 15 or 16, shouldn't they have ridden in a car and actually seen the wheel being used?"

Janice and I have worked together and our families have been friends for 30 years. I learned from her drive partner that she hadn't driven before driver education class. On her first drive, she made the turn and then drove up onto a yard, taking out the bushes before coming to a stop.

The teacher said, "Why didn't you bring the wheel back after your turn?" Just like Janice, she said, "Because you didn't tell me to." Like mother, like daughter; when I taught Amy, her daughter, a farm girl, she hadn't driven before class either.

One time I was driving weekends in Davenport. Three of the eight students had no concept of how a steering wheel worked.

Their entire first hour was spent in the parking lot doing figure eights learning how to operate a steering wheel.

Steering comes first. If students don't understand that, you can't proceed to the brake or accelerator. Most people use hand-over-hand steering. The other option is what is called push-pull steering. Whichever they use, it is important to be able to make the turn smoothly.

Sometimes new drivers don't understand that you must let the wheel return or else you go up on to the sidewalk or, worse yet, onto someone's lawn.

Practice for young people on a riding mower is a great place to start. It is pretty obvious if you can drive a straight path or make a clean turn. One friend would not let his children even think about driver education until they could show they mastered mowing the lawn. That was a great idea considering he had a big yard.

A big empty parking lot is another great place to work on young people's driving skills. Some rural parents start on the local gravel roads where there is plenty of room and little traffic. Others start driving in the cemetery rather than in quiet residential neighborhoods.

Off-Road Recovery

It was my first summer teaching driver education. I was riding with Ruth and her instructor. This girl was petrified and should not have been taking driver's education. Tammy, her teacher, could not get her to drive on the highway over 40 mph and she was drifting all over the road. The mother, too afraid and unwilling to drive with Ruth, decided she should have a professional teach her.

Our policy requires we always have three people in the car for liability reasons. This is why I was asked to ride along. Maybe the girl's drive partner didn't show up for her lesson because she was too frightened—she had ridden with Ruth before.

As we were driving down the road, the instructor told Ruth she was going to do an off-road recovery. This was to be the first I had ever witnessed. I'm pretty sure this girl had no idea what that was. The teacher grabbed the wheel, pulling the car onto the shoulder at 40 mph as the gravel flew.

Now I was the one who was terrified. I was in the back seat with no brake or steering wheel.

When the lesson was over and we arrived safely back at school, I asked Tammy, "What was that all about?" She replied, "Because this girl is going to be on the shoulder regularly, she more than anyone needed to know how to save herself.

Years ago Phil and Noel used to teach braking and off-road recovery in case of an emergency. They had the student drive at 55 mph. On the teacher's command, the student was to slow to 25 mph as fast as possible, then pull the car safely onto the shoulder.

One day after practicing this procedure, they crested a hill on Old Highway 61. Lying in the road was a man in a suit. His top leg was figure-four over the bottom. They quickly slowed and pulled off.

Upon stopping, they realized it was a suit of clothes. As they investigated, a car came backing over the crest of the hill looking for the garments its driver had lost off the top of the car.

John and students were working on off-road recoveries one day on the Humeston Road north of DeWitt. The shoulder wasn't wide enough and they were stuck. Being a country boy himself, he asked the neighboring farmer to pull them out. This saved a fortune on wrecker fees.

It did require several car washes to get all the mud removed.

New drivers have a tendency to overcorrect, or jerk the wheel. This happens when they try to keep the vehicle from drifting, or when the right wheel hits the shoulder of the road. This sometimes causes rollovers, which account for about 25 percent of all fatal crashes, because occupants, usually teens, aren't seatbelted.[19]

Overcorrecting is one of the leading causes of teen fatalities in Iowa. Lack of experience is the main reason; the more a person drives, the less this happens.

We used to teach off-road recovery, the procedure for bringing the car back up onto the pavement when the right wheels hit the shoulder. Everyone at some time accidentally drifts off the pavement onto the gravel. Anyone who claims otherwise is a beginner or liar.

Off-road recovery is a skill all drivers should master. Our university instructors insist this is too dangerous to carry out with novice drivers in a driver education car. We do cover the topic in the classroom.

This is how it used to work. We selected a quiet two-lane highway that had wide, dry shoulders, and good visibility.

The instructor in the passenger seat positions the left hand on the steering wheel and eases the car onto the shoulder while going 25-35 mph. The first time, the teacher brings the car back up onto the pavement. All the while, the student hands are placed at 10 o'clock and 2 o'clock in order to feel the car's movements and its vibrations on and off the shoulder.

Twice more the instructor maneuvers the car onto the shoulder. Each time the student gradually pulls the car back up onto the road. As soon as the car goes off the pavement, students should take their foot off the accelerator and not touch the brake, either.

Chapter 5: Bad Decisions
"You did what?!"

Alcohol and other drugs

One spring when we were kids, my Dad was walking down the highway on the north side of our farm. He was picking asparagus and was quite surprised when he discovered a cache of beer someone had hidden in the ditch. He had no idea whom it might have belonged to. Not a drinker, Dad didn't understand the value of this commodity when he gave it away.

My older brother and his high school buddies were camping in our woods that night. They were pretty disappointed when they learned they were going to be without refreshments.

Each Sunday morning Dad would get so irritated when he had to pick up a beer can in our ditch. This lasted for a couple of summers. It stopped as suddenly as it had started. We could only guess the person died, lost his license, his job, sobered up, or got transferred. If we had known how long it took to drink a beer, maybe we could have calculated which bar the person was coming from.

Paula told of her driver education instructor with an ever-present coffee mug in his hand. This drink didn't help him relax because his constant screaming had both boys and girls in tears. The back seat students were certain they were going to die the day their timid driver rolled onto Interstate 80 while multiple semis charged. To the relief of all, the teacher was fired in the middle of the session when school administrators discovered his drink was spiked Irish coffee.

In the late 1970s, Jim was hoping to survive the driver education class he took during the summertime. His two partners, both guys, would come early and smoke marijuana before their drives. With red, bloodshot eyes, both would enter the car smelling like pot. The instructor was a big, excitable guy who was not very observant.

Driver No. 1 almost took out an old lady crossing the intersection at the stop sign by the Iowa Mutual building in DeWitt. The teacher crushed the brake, demanding to know why the driver didn't stop. The answer was simple. He hadn't seen the woman or the sign.

Another day they were practicing off-road recoveries, the procedure where students bring the car back onto the road after the right wheels veer onto the gravel shoulder. This is a dangerous maneuver even for an alert driver at the recommended speed of 25-35 mph.

Driver No. 2 was headed east of DeWitt on Old Highway 30. At 55 mph, this guy pulls off the road onto the gravel and then down into the ditch. Jim didn't know what saved them, either the teacher's screams or his own praying in the back seat. To Jim's amazement, these stoned guys both passed driver education.

When my daughter Whitney was in high school, she played soccer for a neighboring school. In the late 1990s, some schools had some pretty lenient substance policies. Apparently they weren't really serious about ending alcohol and drug use by their teenage athletes. At the junior-senior prom, one of her teammates was arrested for possession of cocaine.

This girl was suspended from play for a total of 1.5 games. This was 11% of the season. In football, if you got in trouble, you only missed one game out of their nine-game schedule. Whit was really upset that the school didn't take a more serious stand against substance abuse among its student athletes.

My son, Ty, was an accomplished runner. He had the good fortune of having great coaches in cross country and track during high school, at UW–La Crosse University, and at Wartburg College.

His high school cross country team went undefeated for two seasons, winning back-to-back state titles. His junior year they won the state meet by 80 points, with five runners scoring in the top 21.

The track team was a Top 10 team for several years. As seniors they were excited about their chance to also win the state meet in this sport. They had the top 4 x 800 team. Tyler had finished 2nd in the two-mile race and 5th in the mile race the previous year.

The week before the state meet, Tyler attended a graduation party for a friend and classmate of 13 years. The parents foolishly let the kids drink. After collecting everyone's car keys, they put them on the dresser next to the front door. After Tyler had a few drinks, he spotted his keys and left. Later, a deputy found him sleeping in his car in a roadside ditch.

Ty didn't come home that night and missed the Mass the next morning that celebrated all our church's graduating seniors. He had been arrested for OWI, Operating While Intoxicated, and was in the Clinton County jail. He had broken his school's conduct code, and wasn't eligible to run at state the following weekend. His team didn't score in any of the three events for which Tyler had qualified, and they lost the state meet by eight points.

Tyler's coach had spent years building a track powerhouse, working with Ty and his friends since 7th grade. This was his chance to bring home a first-place trophy, but it was not to be.

Skater's appearance seemed a bit odd. At age 17, he had a shaved head and wore an ace bandage on his right wrist and hand. Neither hampered his driving, so nothing was said.

Later I learned from the other instructor that Skater had been beaten up in a bar parking lot by a guy 38 years old. He couldn't remove the gravel from his scalp, so he cut off all his hair. He carried two knives with him while in the driver's education car; the shortest blade was six inches long. According to Skater, these were his protection the next time he got into a fight when he was out drinking.

Skater existed in an environment that didn't produce success. He was a student at the alternative high school, which has since closed due to 45% attendance and a dismal graduation rate of 30%.

He demonstrated his irresponsibility and immaturity in numerous ways. Though his driving skills were adequate, he was aggressive and cocky. This type, usually boys, never improve. Why would you ever need to teach or coach someone who thinks he knows everything? He displayed his surly attitude whenever suggestions for improvement were given.

Skater skipped one scheduled drive after a hard night; 9 a.m. was too early to expect him to get out of bed. Another time we had to cross the Mississippi River to find his driving permit. He had stayed at his girlfriend's place the night before in Illinois and left it behind. He also missed one classroom session because of a court appearance. Naively, I assumed court and the hand wrap were related to the bar fight.

Two years later I had Shea as a student driver. Her parents were hard-working immigrants who owned the convenience store half a block from the public high school. She shared the rest of the story about Skater, and coincidentally why they had their business up for sale.

As it turned out, both the court date and the ace bandage had nothing to do with the bar fight. Skater had broken into Shea's family's station and had stolen $10,000 worth of cigarettes, that is, about 200 cartons. He lacerated his hand and wrist when he smashed through the front door. The wrap covered up the resulting stitches. The robbery is what necessitated his day in court two years prior.

You are probably thinking, I pray I never meet this kid on a dark, narrow, two-lane highway, driving a 3,000-pound weapon after he's had too much to drink and just had a fight with his girlfriend.

You don't need to worry; Shea assured me that Skater's significant police record is going to keep him incarcerated for a long time.

The story above is true. Unfortunately there are students on the road not only unprepared for driving but unprepared for life. The consequences can be deadly. With time and education, I hope this will improve.

One summer I had a big class of more than 40 students who met every weekday morning from 7 to 9 a.m. Jake skipped several classes, and thought he could sleep through the ones he did attend. When students skip class or drives, they are required to pay extra fees. His bill added up quickly. After he had skipped his fourth class out of a total of 15, I told him he was expelled.

He got mad, cursed, and crumpled up the fake medical excuse written by his mother. This was supposed to pardon his fourth miss. I knew no real doctor would ever schedule a boy 16 for a 7 a.m. summer appointment.

After consulting with my boss, I did let him finish the class. Because of his missed classes, though, Jake had to pay the extra $100. He also had to finish his last two classes in a town 30 minutes away, and he got stamped. This meant he was required to take the drive with the DOT examiners. In Iowa, most students receive a driver's license without being required to take a state drive test. What a shame for Jake, technically a very good driver. That's what drug use, lack of sleep, and a surly attitude will get you.

You might ask why I stamp a student with a bad attitude. Using my best judgment, I have a responsibility to put safe drivers on the highway. No one wants a selfish teenager with anger issues driving.

Jordan was in a crash last fall in the Illinois Quad Cities. She, her sister, a friend, and boyfriend who was 19 went haunted housing. The friend let the young man drive her car. Driving recklessly, he lost control, and he hit and seriously injured two pedestrians. Then he hit a pole and a tree that stopped the car from rolling down a steep embankment.

When the police arrived, they soon learned the guy had no license and was in possession of marijuana. Jordan was thankful that the guy admitted his ownership. So all three girls were released and not charged. The guy is now serving time. Because of her poor judgment, the owner of the car is now an ex-girlfriend with a wrecked vehicle.

Grandma and Grandpa are Jordan's guardians. Now she is not allowed to go anywhere with someone they have not met. She said they are great and she appreciates the new house rules.

Snail and Joe Drunk are employed at the same factory as my sister-in-law near Madison, Wis. Snail can't understand why he got his nickname. At age 23 his brain is fried from too much dope. He is so slow it is an effort for him to turn his head.

Besides being non-productive, he is always bumming a ride to and from work.

Joe Drunk usually taxis Snail, but requires him to pay for his rides each week. This puts gas in the car and helps pay for Drunk's habit. One night after work, Snail paid Joe $10.

Snail was instructed to put gas in the tank as soon as Joe was finished prepaying. Standing next to the vehicle, he couldn't remember why he had gotten out of the car.

After leaving the station, Joe noticed the gas gauge was still on empty. When questioning Snail, he learned that his passenger forgot to put fuel in.

They went back, but by this time another customer was using the pump. Plus the machine no longer had the $10 credit on it. So Joe had to wait in line to start the whole process over again. He was not too pleased with his rider.

Recently, sitting down the table from my sister-in-law, Snail bit into his sandwich during their lunch break. Something wasn't right. After he took the second bite, he realized he hadn't taken the plastic off the piece of cheese in his sandwich.

Joe is 55 but looks long past retirement age. He has a breath alcohol ignition interlock device in his car. These are often required for drivers after they have been arrested for drunk driving. These prevent inebriated people from starting their car. For the engine to start, a sober driver is required to blow into the machine.

Joe has been left stranded after work on four occasions when his car refused to start. Each time it cost him about $150 to reactivate the ignition device so when he is sober he can operate his vehicle.

Joe also wears a GPS ankle bracelet so the authorities know his whereabouts at all times. At work on numerous occasions it started buzzing; the mechanism was alerting him that the batteries needed charging. It isn't unusual to see Joe during work and on breaks standing by the wall with his leg plugged into a socket for re-charging. This is so his probation officer doesn't think he is AWOL.

Two of my former students, both minors, died in a car crash. Several months later there was an ad in the paper offering a $5,000 reward to whoever provided information leading to the arrest and conviction of whoever supplied the alcohol that contributed to the deaths of these two young people.

One Friday night when I was 19, a young couple was celebrating the wife's graduation from nursing school, with her parents. In two cars they were traveling south on Highway 31, the main route connecting Racine and Kenosha. Our farm's front yard was on the curve of this road.

At 11 p.m. we were awakened by a thunderous noise. Two cars landed in our front yard. An intoxicated northbound lady had crossed over the centerline, barely missing the first car carrying the young couple.

The parents who were following weren't so lucky.

We worked to remove the victims from the wreckage while waiting for the emergency vehicles to arrive. We never learned if any of the three survived. This was in 1972, the summer before I started college. I will never forget this tragedy.

For decades drunk driving was a plague for which people believed there wasn't much of a cure. That all changed with Candy Lightner, founder of the organization Mothers Against

Drunk Driving. This organization advocated stiffer drunk driving penalties and for the legal drinking age to be raised to 21.

MADD lobbied at all levels. The public took notice and legislation was passed. There were finally severe consequences for drunk driving.[20]

In 1980 drinking-and-driving-related fatalities were 60% of all highway deaths. By 2011 they were 32% nationally, in Iowa 26%.[21]

Today, being arrested while intoxicated has serious consequences. A drunk driving arrest stays on your record for 12 years. A drug arrest stays on your record for the rest of your life.

Parents, don't serve minors, even if it is your teen's graduation party. Supplying a minor with alcohol can result in jail time and big fines for you. If someone is injured or killed, the supplier, when convicted, will spend years in prison. In civil court, you could lose a fortune, plus your home, business, or farm.

Some states have legalized marijuana. According to a trooper friend, "THC stays in your system up to 30 days, affecting your judgment and driving performance. If they want to make pot legal, then just don't let these smokers have a driver's license."

Poor Choices

With no inhibitions, Matt was a maniac in a car. If the speed sign on the curve said 50 mph, he was sure he could take it at 70. Stop sign—What was that? He was fun, the life of the party. The only thing worse than his driving was that we got in the car with him. He has been at the last two high school class reunions. He is still Mr. Irresponsibility. I don't know how many jobs Matt has had, but he has been married four times. He explained, "I really like being married, I'm just not very good at it." Frankly, I am amazed he is still alive.

Barbara, one of my driver's ed students, was living alone in a small town several miles from school. She hated it. "No one works, and all they do is drink and hunt," she said. That seems like a dangerous combination.

Her parents are truckers who were gone most of the time. Big sister was supposed to be staying with her, but she was always at her boyfriend's place.

Barbara, 17, has been in seven crashes, one while riding a dirt bike, two while driving a four-wheeler. Her sister, 19, has already had five crashes, four in which she was the passenger.

I asked, "Do think it is such a good idea for you to be riding with your sister?" The reply was, "I know she is a terrible driver, but she would never hurt me."

Last August, a friend, Tony, shared this story as we were giving blood at the local high school.

Soon after his son turned 16 and got his license, he and his girlfriend crashed into a bridge on a curvy street near their home.

The pair had gone to a movie. About an hour after the show let out, they called Dad informing him that they had hit a train viaduct in the quieter part of town.

Tony arrived at the scene and surveyed the damage before anyone else came. Thankfully, no one was hurt. After some contemplation, his only advice to the young couple was, "Honey, you'd better get your blouse turned right side out before the police get here." Her deer insignia on the front of her shirt was backward and on the opposite side.

The next day his son asked, "Dad, how did you know?"

The soft reply was, "I was once a teenager."

One boy, 17, who was not a very good driver, said, "Both my parents are bad drivers, but they both gave me the same piece of advice."

"What was that?" I asked.

"The No. 1 most important thing about driving is, watch for cops."

There was an old cabin in our woods. It was two converted chicken coops that a Boy Scout troop had remodeled about 10 years earlier. We fixed it up and had a great place to sleep and hang out when we were in high school.

Most of us were not yet 16, when one Saturday night Frank and Dean decided they were going to walk the couple of miles into town for something to eat. On their way back, some beautiful sirens invited them in for a drink.

Tim, newly 16, arrived at the cabin in his beige-colored Ford Fairlane coupe just a few minutes before Frank and Dean returned. They shared a tale that was hard to believe. So six dumb kids piled into Tim's car, praying this wasn't a snipe hunt, yet hoping for some action.

Sure enough, the house was real. We stopped and knocked on the door. By this time the girls' boyfriends were back. They screamed at us to leave. I don't remember all of what was said. I do recall it being like a Three Stooges movie with six guys trying to climb into the little two-door all at once. We sped away with two bad a---- in hot pursuit driving an old Dodge. Tim hit 85 mph, quite a feat for his little car with a thousand pounds of passengers.

Eventually, our pursuers pulled alongside the Fairlane and rammed the back left panel, trying to run us off the road. At this point someone said, "What if they have a gun?" Instantly, six bodies tried to lower themselves from view below the windows. This was the most scared I had ever been in my life.

When we got back to our farm drive, Tim whipped the car into our driveway and shut off the lights. Our pursuers couldn't quite make the turn. As we pulled by our house, Dean jumped out. We drove back behind the house and then down to the woods using our farm lane. These guys drove around our barnyard a couple of times without spotting anyone, then left.

We waited until we thought the coast was clear. We snuck back up to the house looking for Dean. He was lying on the south porch of the house behind the big bridal wreath bushes moaning. "They got me. They got me. I think I'm going to die!" At this point I said, "That's it, we have to wake up my parents to take him to the hospital."

Instantly, Dean jumped to his feet and replied, "Oh, shucks, I was just kidding." He should have been thankful that we didn't kill him on the spot. We quietly returned to the cabin, all thankful to be alive.

The next day Dad couldn't figure out how his mailbox had gotten knocked off the post. No one was talking. A couple of months later my brother returned on leave from the Army. He thought we should go confront these guys.

He had no takers.

About five years ago Jill shared this story about her farm boy brother. "Paul is a 21-year-old who is engaged to be married. He and his fiancée are buying a house together. She is 31, and also our third cousin."

I asked, "Does she have any children?"

"She had a couple, but I think they were taken away. Mom and Dad haven't been too happy during this whole affair. What really put them over the edge is when they learned that this woman tried to poison her ex-boyfriend!"

The following letter I intended to have put on the editorial pages of the following newspapers: The Kenosha News, Racine Journal, and the Milwaukee Journal Sentinel. Chancellor Ford wrote a nice response letter, although I didn't agree with her arguments, and I chose not to take any further action.

March 24, 2014

Dear Chancellor Deborah Ford:

On Sunday, March 16, we went to see the performance "How I Learned to Drive" at UW-Parkside. I am a semi-retired driver's education teacher. When we saw the attractive ad in the Kenosha News, we thought this would be a fun production to see.

In tiny print it said mature audience. I thought that it was referring to some of the off-color humor. It didn't announce it was actually a play about the repeated rape of a young girl.

We were visiting my parents for the weekend, both in their 90s. They don't have the Internet. So we were unable to learn the theme of this play before we attended.

When I asked at the ticket office if this was a comedy, the young woman said there were some funny parts. If she had shared what the play was about, I would not have wasted $36 on this disgusting performance. I believe I was lied to, both by your advertising and ticket seller.

There were probably 75 people in the small theater. Approximately one-fourth of the audience was elderly. I am certain that any senior who understood the content was offended.

My question is: Why weren't the producers of the production truthful about the topic of this play? Some may consider this material sophisticated. The vast majority of our population wouldn't. That is why they had to make it appear to be something other than what it was.

This play had nothing to do with learning to drive. It was a vulgar production about the incestuous rape of an 11-year-old girl by her uncle, which continued for seven years. I was terribly disappointed.

I have family members who perform in theater. I know they work very hard at their craft. The UW-Parkside performers were very talented. It is a shame they didn't have an opportunity to perform for an audience that could fully appreciate their skills.

I hope the University Of Wisconsin-Parkside doesn't condone this type of deception in advertising. Please consider the poor judgment someone used in the promotion of this play. Let me know what actions were taken so Parkside's reputation isn't tarnished further.

I come from a huge family, with hundreds of relatives and friends. Most live in Kenosha, Racine, and Milwaukee. None will be pleased if they learn that Parkside supports deception in advertising.

—Bill Mueller, Driver's Education Teacher

Emotions

In 10 years of working with student drivers, I had never experienced a crying driver. Last July, Woodrow, our other instructor, at the end of a long afternoon, shared his experience with Mia. She was going to be a senior in the fall. In the middle of an intersection she let go of the steering wheel and started bawling. Then she started doing deep breathing exercises to stop her panic attack.

The very next day on our second lesson, Alex drove to Princeton where we switched drivers. Pulling from the Casey's convenience store onto Highway 67, a quiet road, Kara began to cry. I asked, "What's wrong!"

She said, "I'm not ready to drive on the highway."

We pulled into the closest driveway and then had Alex drive back to school. We spent the next hour driving in the school parking lot and on nearby residential streets. When I realized how unprepared she was to be behind the wheel, it was my turn to cry. Sitting behind Kara in the driver education car was most harrowing for Alex. He had no brake to stomp or steering wheel to grab as I did.

Upon our return to school I explained to her mother that Kara needed to practice. She was required to drive 20 hours, not counting her six hours with me. Her score today was 50%, a gift. Later in the day, her Mom called my boss explaining that Kara wasn't ready and would take a later class. I'm not sure who was most relieved, Alex or I.

Two weeks later a third girl, Haley, on her final drive, started wailing, not once but twice.

In Iowa, any student not ready to drive alone is required to take the drive test with the DOT upon completion of driver's education.

I tell all students numerous times that if their driving grade is under 80%, they will be required to drive with the DOT. At the end of six drives, Haley's average was in the low 70s. At the end of every drive she received a copy of her drive score for that day, with numerous suggestions for improvement.

On our final session, she practiced parallel parking. Knowing Haley was going to have to take the drive test, I wanted her to be proficient at it. That is one of the test requirements and for most students the scariest.

The procedure is quite simple and most students learn quickly. This was Haley's third parking lesson and it wasn't going so well. She bawled, "I am never going to be able to parallel park!"

Haley was a straight-A student who worked very hard in school. I don't know why with less than two hours of driving experience, not counting her time in the driver education car, she thought she would be successful.

It is not a pleasant experience for students to learn they have to take the DOT drive test, or for me when I inform them of the impending drive test.

I always ask, "Do you believe you are ready to drive by yourself?" They always agree they aren't. When I asked Haley that question she erupted with, "I will never be able to drive by myself!" Each time Haley drove, Shane her drive partner, was captive in the back seat for a frightening hour. He must have been as shocked as I with Haley's response at having to take the DOT drive test.

While driving with Mr. Batey in June, Michelle was backed into in a Dubuque parking lot. We then learned that the previous weekend she was rear-ended at an intersection. A victim of two crashes in less than a week, she was pretty shaken. Only the driver's side door of the driver education car was damaged. She thought her back was a little sore and wasn't sure if she should go back out so soon. Mr. Batey, to his credit, told her they could open the driver's door so it wasn't a real serious crash. He got her back behind the wheel right away.

John, the father of one of my students, shared this story. Fifteen years ago he was a young Lowden farmer who was also working an off-the-farm job in Cedar Rapids. Coming home he almost rear-ended a car that had no brake lights or turn signal, sitting in the road. He may have been waiting to make a left turn. Avoiding the crash, he also blasted his horn as he went by. In a rage, the other driver sped ahead in the left lane alongside John, lowered his right window, and pointed a 45 revolver at John's head. Shocked, John slammed on his brakes, and thankfully the maniac and his junker drove out of sight.

One Saturday in South Lake, Texas, next door to Grapevine, my son, Ty, and I saw a bicyclist in a rage. This guy was all decked out in a fancy riding suit and helmet, standing next to his bike in the middle of the median. As we approached, he threw a rock at a car speeding away. I can only guess the vehicle's driver forced the bike off the road and into the grass in the middle of four lanes of traffic.

In Leander, Texas, about four years ago, we were driving down a four-lane residential street with a big median down the middle. A young lady behind us started honking her horn to get our attention. Just as we were pulling through the stop sign, a guy in another vehicle forced her car up onto the curb. He pulled her out of her car and hit her to the ground. It took a minute to get turned around and back to the scene. When we returned both the people and the cars had disappeared. We don't know the cause or the result of the assault, but we did witness anger.

A couple of years ago an off-duty police officer in eastern Iowa was driving in Davenport. Upset, she flashed her gun, trying to intimidate another driver. Consequently, she lost her job.

One officer said when he was young his Dad told him, "You may not always be able to avoid a ticket, but you sure can talk yourself into one."

"Today," the officer said, "you wouldn't believe the curses I sometimes get when pulling over people who have just violated a law."

He also noted how much tougher it is to write a ticket when the person is really nice. Officers always appreciate a wave from other motorists. That is, if they use all their fingers. He said, "We already know we are No. 1."

I met Sheena, recently working for my friend. She took driver education in the 1980s in a small eastern Iowa town. Her driving instructor was tall and mean, and he had a big belly.

They drove with three students in a car with a bench seat. Sheena was short, so each day she was the designated last driver. The teacher's legs would fall asleep every time she drove and frequent stops were required for him to get the blood circulating.

One of her drive partners was a farm boy who had been driving most of his life. Mike was really intimidated by this man. On his first drive he was instructed to put the car in gear to leave the parking space. He put it in drive and ran the car into the side of the school building.

On the second day the instructor, being a real problem solver, had the car turned around with the back end facing the building. He told Mike to put the car in gear and pull out. This time, in a state of panic, Mike shifted into reverse and smashed the car into the building a second time.

Jerry, a former co-worker, told of his driver education teacher in California. When asked, "Who are better drivers, boys or girls?" he wouldn't say, but he did explain how they react differently.

Boys in an emergency will put a death grip on the wheel, and girls will let go altogether and grab their head with both hands. I had a girl driver take both hands off the steering wheel. That's when I grabbed it to control the car.

Often there is debate between boys and girls as to who are the better drivers. Boys will destroy their car all at once; two-thirds of all teen fatalities are caused by male drivers. That is why their insurance premiums are higher. Girls destroy their vehicles one fender at a time.

Some time ago I had two girl softball players, both ninth graders playing freshman ball. I asked about the team and its talent fielding. Then I asked how good their bats were, meaning the team's batters. The driver answered that being the youngest team in the high school, they had the oldest equipment with only a couple of good bats.

Her drive partner in the back seat was laughing through this explanation because she understood the question. As we were driving down the highway, our driver realized that I was asking about the team's hitting. In her embarrassment, she took her hands off the wheel—You guessed it!—and put them on her head.

Good drivers let you know what their intentions are. When we see motorists who don't drive safely we tend to get irritated. This can affect our ability to make good decisions. I tell my students just don't get mad.

Any time you see someone drive dangerously or erratically, give yourself more space. It isn't your job to get even. Be positive; you don't know what might be going on in that person's life.

Or it may be they suffer from a malady called HUB. This is Head Up Butt disease. Don't get upset, just smile, and do what you need to do to stay safe.

Even with that said, I still sometimes enjoy the guilty pleasure of pretending I am Elizabeth Montgomery in the old TV show, *Bewitched.* I wrinkle my nose and the menace and car drive into the ditch.

According to the American Automobile Association, aggressive driving is driving without regard for others' safety, and road rage is driving with the intent to harm others. You never know what someone in a rage is capable of. Don't make eye contact with them. If your driver ever starts to lose it, either switch drivers or get them to stop and cool off.

Anxiety is another strong emotion. Fear can make it more difficult to concentrate and identify hazards. When possible, try to avoid stressful circumstances.

Entitled

At one rural school several students warned me about spoiled Blake, age 14, who wasn't going to behave in my class. According to them he was in the school office every day for his delinquency. In driver's education class he was actually well behaved.

The problem was that Blake was a poor driver who needed a lot more practice. After every drive, I gave him his drive score for that day. They were all in the 60s and 70s. Throughout our six drives, I kept reminding him that he needed at least an 80% driving grade. With anything less he would be stamped and required to take the drive test with the DOT examiner. Sure enough, on our last day when he received his certificate stamped, he had a tantrum. This once he didn't get his way.

I have repeatedly told one mother I see at the YMCA she needs to be practicing with her daughter before she takes driver's ed. Mom informed me, "Dad is going to have to drive with her from now on."

"What happened?" I asked.

"On Sunday I let her drive me to Davenport to go shopping. When I refused to buy her an expensive sweater, she locked me out of the car. How embarrassing!"

A year ago my drive students told me of a girl in their class. Her parents bought her an $80,000 car upon completion of driver education. Is that possible?

Many students either have jobs to pay for their own driver education or are in various extracurricular activities. When they have drive-time conflicts, I try to adjust schedules for their convenience. I asked a girl if she for one day would be willing to move her 11 a.m. drive time to 9 a.m. Her answer was, "No!" She could not get out of bed that early on a Saturday morning.

More recently other students told me of a senior who for graduation was given a new Lamborghini. This is a kid I taught driver education to a couple of years ago.

He was troubled then and according to the boys, in their words, "He is still not normal. Last year he attended a military school. It didn't help." They also said the parents, who are well off, bought a place in a Southern state where this kid will live while attending college.

Compare those two with Topher. His Dad is a highly successful local businessman. When he took his driving class, Toph drove from 7 to 9 a.m. on Saturday mornings.

After each drive, his Dad had a work list for him to complete that day. I asked if his folks were going to get him a car. He said he was responsible to buy his own car. Dad would probably help him with the down payment.

Topher was a really nice kid. He was a very good student and involved in many school activities. His work ethic and attitude were great. He did comment on his displeasure with classmates who were given cars by their indulgent parents.

The majority of students put forth a lot of effort to earn a driver's license. Most students would drive in the middle of the night if they could finish driver education sooner.

Unfortunately, we get a few students who feel entitled. They will do nothing to inconvenience themselves. I used to ask my students, "Do you know anyone who is spoiled?" All hands would go up.

I would tell them, "Unless they learn from life's lessons, the entitled, like the spoiled, will never be successful in life."

Don't let a spoiled teen who still has tantrums get a driver's license. There is no limit to the pain and suffering they can cause when you put them in a 3,000-pound automobile.

Some people with horrible parenting skills create spoiled and entitled kids. In many cases it is the parents' fault when their offspring don't become responsible contributing citizens.

Chapter 6: Highways and Byways

Expressways

On a couple of occasions we have had semis with room to move over just playing with us, to see what we would do. That would cost big-time if an officer caught them messing with a driver education car.

Phil's student driver was driving south of DeWitt on Highway 61. A car was entering from the East Highway 30 ramp. Phil told the student to speed up to get ahead of a lady who was not paying attention to the traffic coming along beside her. The boy didn't speed up. Instead, without looking, he swerved into the path of the left lane traffic. Phil jerked the car back as the woman finally saw them. She hit her brakes causing her car to fishtail before going into a 360-degree spin. Traffic in both directions started taking the shoulder. The driver education car finally got stopped up the road a ways. Phil's driver was pretty shaken up.

The lady who caused this whole affair stopped and wanted to call the police and exchange insurance information in case her wheels or alignment were damaged.

About this time a traffic enforcement officer pulled up and informed the lady that her suggestion wouldn't be necessary. This was a good "look over your shoulder lesson" for both the beginner and the lady with 25 years of driving experience.

One person I play Sheepshead cards with told of his grandson taking driver education at North Scott High School, in

Eldridge, Iowa. This was when students took the class during the school day.

The teacher and students were driving west on Interstate 80. The teacher told the driver not to turn around until he was told to. Soon the instructor fell asleep and they reached Iowa City, an hour away from school, before he awakened. I don't think they were back in time for their next class.

Last September I heard another version of that same story. This was a middle-aged father telling about the intimidating football coach-driver education instructor in the Quad Cities years ago. Again, the driver education car was heading west on Interstate 80. This time the students were all afraid to wake the teacher when he fell asleep. Again they reached Iowa City an hour from home.

I did check with friends Phil and Rodney, who both are fellow driving instructors. They assured me both stories were true. They gave me the names of both nappers and the names of others who could collaborate the stories. It would be interesting to know how many schools have this or similar legends.

Back before cell phones, Ernie tells the story about leaving his wife behind. They were coming home late one night. She was sleeping in the back seat under a blanket. He pulled into a wayside oasis to use the men's room. While he was stopped, she awoke and decided she needed to use the ladies' room. When she returned, he and the car were gone. He never said how long it took for him to realize he no longer had a passenger, or how this affected their marital bliss.

Timmy, a friend from Tennessee, was a young, broke high school science teacher. For extra income he also drove a school bus. This created so much stress in his life he said he used to have this recurring nightmare. "I dreamt that I died, and was sent to hell. My punishment was that I was going to have to drive school bus for all eternity." Timmy is a fun guy with a great sense of humor. He likes to pick and then see how people are going to react, the way Andy of Mayberry used to pick at Barney in the old *Andy Griffith Show*. One night he and his wife, Leslie, were driving home in a torrential storm. He started to critique her driving; he started to pick.

"It wasn't much," he said, but when Leslie had enough, she slammed on the brakes, almost putting him through the windshield.

"Get out!" she said, "You are going to drive the rest of the way home."

When he opened the door and got out to exchange drivers, his new suit was soaked in seconds. Leslie, in her anger, sped away along the road and then stopped. He walked the 200 yards to get back in when she took off again. He never said how many miles he walked that night, but he was cured of picking for a while.

Another time he and a friend were coming home late from a business trip. Pete, his passenger, was fast asleep and Timmy was feeling his normal orneriness. He pulled into a truck stop and drove in front of a semi parked with its headlights on. Timmy slammed on his brakes and screamed, "Oh, my God!"

Pete nearly died of a heart attack, while Timmy laughed. It took several minutes for Pete to bring his heart rate under control. After threatening to kill his driver, he vowed to never close his eyes again in a car driven by Timmy. They made it home wide awake.

I frequently tell my students to be alert for the crazies out there. In July we encountered four in one day. The first two were driving pickups south on Highway 61. We were trying to pass a car that wasn't holding a consistent speed. Along came these two guys doing 75 in a 65 mph zone. From the right, the first guy cut us off, and then the second truck did the same. We hit our brake and our horn, barely avoiding a crash. I guess this maniac never saw the STUDENT DRIVER sign before he flipped us off.

A couple of hours later, we were preparing to turn left from Devils Glen Road onto Belmont St. going back to Pleasant Valley High School. We signaled, and as we moved into the center turn lane, a guy passed us on the left.

Later that same afternoon we were exiting Interstate 74 onto Interstate 80 going west. The ramp goes from two lanes to one. A car passed us as his lane ended, missing us by inches.

President Dwight Eisenhower signed the Federal Aid Highway Act of 1956. The Federal Government picked up 90% of the cost. The goal was to improve our national security. We wanted to move military convoys quickly if attacked during the Cold War.[22]

Even though expressways are safer than other highways, they can be tricky to drive because of the high speeds and sheer number of cars.

Interchanges can be dangerous. In my opinion, the cloverleaf is the worst. Often there are several cars trying to enter and exit at the same time with little room to maneuver. Some exiting cars slow but don't signal, making it more difficult for the vehicles entering from the ramp. Making your intentions known to other drivers is key, so use those signals.

I tell my students to stay in their lane until they know it is safe and clear to move left into the moving highway traffic. Don't stop. If there is no gap to safely fit in then drive up the shoulder until there is one. If you stop, you become a hazard for the people behind you as well as for the vehicles traveling in excess of 70 mph on the expressway.

Once on the expressway, drive the speed of the other traffic, if it is not exceeding the speed limit. Know your route, concentrate on the driving task, and stay alert.

Multi-lane roads look like interstate highways with speeds as high as 65 to 70 mph. The difference is they have intersections and allow slow-moving vehicles such as farm implements to use the roadway.

Rural Driving

One of Bethany's two drive partners, not knowing how to correct the wheel, landed the car in the tall grass 20 feet off the road. The instructor drove the car back up onto the road, put the novice back behind the wheel, then explained the correct procedure. When he thought she was ready, she started up again and then drove the car into the ditch a second time.

To this day, Andria is still nervous on gravel and never exceeds 35 mph. She grew up in western Iowa. Driver's education classes used to be taught during the regular school day. She was at a Leadership Conference and missed the first few days of her class.

Andria had never been behind the wheel of a car before. On her first day, her young instructor had her on a gravel road, but not for long. Andria overcorrected the wheel after hitting the shoulder, which caused the car to roll three times.

When the car landed on its top, the instructor and she were suspended upside down from their shoulder harnesses. For some reason, the girl in the back seat wasn't wearing a belt but fortunately wasn't injured. Over the next five years, 17 of her 33 classmates had car crashes. She was sad that her instructor lasted only one year, not entirely sure of the reason for his short teaching career.

With no streetlights, it was at first difficult for John, a Chicago native, to drive on Iowa's dark rural roadways. We were both students at Loras College.

Once we took a road trip to Southern Illinois University to see Red, my college roommate of three years. He was a law student there. We came across a common rural highway scent. It was the most awful smell John had ever encountered, and which he couldn't identify. It was a skunk.

I ran into a student I had a year-and-a-half ago at the local school's blood drive. She is a second semester junior planning to graduate early in December. I asked her how her driving was going. She said she had two crashes. I asked if they were contributive or her fault; either would make her start her one-year intermediate license over. No, for the first one she hit a cow after dark. For the second, she was rear-ended at a stop sign by someone texting. She said, "It really was a wake-up call."

Leo's hired man, Joe, stole my brother Mike's car. Joe had expressed an interest in buying Mike's old car. Unexpectedly one autumn rainy night he showed up at our door. He asked if he could test drive Mike's car. He said he had the money and was ready to have his own wheels.

The timing seemed odd, but we lived on a major two-lane highway and Dad was used to helping people at all hours. With the keys, Joe was gone.

A few minutes later the police showed up at our door looking for Joe. He had just been arrested at Leo's farm; Leo had various misfits in his employ over many years. Joe had asked the police if he could go back into Leo's house, as he had forgotten his wallet.

He blasted out the back door and up through the field a quarter mile to our house, where he finagled the car keys from us. The next day the car was discovered abandoned a mile from our farm. He never did buy the car.

Once in high school driving down Highway 20 I saw a bag of concrete lying in the road. I put it between my wheels, hoping to straddle it. Unfortunately, it was a little taller than the undercarriage of the car. I left a cloud of dust and the tie rods had to be fixed.

My brother's class was notorious for their escapades in high school. One day, members of the Letterman's Club were going to let a pig out in the gym during the school pep assembly. We were one of the few farm families with kids at St. Cat's in Racine, Wis. My brother was very popular and the instigator of most pranks.

We had only two pigs on our farm. If one had disappeared, the noticeable absence would have been blamed on my brother and his friends, not the staff and attendees at the pep rally. The group decided our neighbor Leo Meier's hog barn would have the appropriate pig. Several cars descended on County Line Road. That was the property line between our two farms.

After bedtime, several of the school's celebrated athletes snuck into Leo's through the woods. The only pigs they discovered were full-sized hogs. Three-hundred pound sows weren't going to fit into their gunnysacks. They did grab some roosting chickens that are always easy to catch after dark. They headed back to the waiting getaway cars.

Meanwhile, a neighbor reported several suspicious cars parked alongside our quiet country road. Back in the 1960s,

Kenosha's sheriff's department cars were Rambler station wagons. By coincidence, this was the same car we owned.

After sprinting 250 yards from the Meier barn, my brother pitched the sack of birds in the backseat of the Rambler and hollered to the driver, "Let's go." At that moment, he suddenly realized he was in the police car.

He escaped by running another quarter of a mile through our cornfield and woods to the house. Though it was a pretty boring assembly the next day, he was happy to learn he was the only member of the band that didn't get hauled to jail the previous night.

Pat was told growing up that if you learned to drive a standard/clutch/stick transmission you could drive anything. She and Bernie decided they were going to make their kids learn with a clutch first. Their children all hated it.

Bernie owned a machining business on the south edge of town, right next to the railroad tracks. Jenny, their oldest, was a classmate of my daughter Whitney. Mom and Dad thought she could practice by circling the shop.

When she got done driving, the front bumper on both sides was dented in, and she lost a piece of the car. Of course, she didn't know how the damage to the vehicle occurred.

We were doing a country drive, on a pretty fall afternoon. Heading to Wheatland, our backseat passenger was quiet and all smiles. I asked her what was up.

"Living in Davenport," a city with a population of 100,000, "I never ever leave the city," she said. "This scenery is awesome, and it's fun seeing all the cows and horses." Being from the country, I take for granted the beautiful landscapes that I see daily.

I was Summer's driving instructor eight or nine years ago. She is one of my daughter Marcy's best friends. Her mother, Patti, shared two of Summer's early calamities.

Three cars were traveling down a rural road when the woman in car No. 1 came to a halt for a box sitting on the pavement. The driver of the second car could see ahead and was able to react appropriately. Following too closely in car three, Summer hit the car ahead. No need to call Dad and Mom; they were in car No. 2.

Her second mishap was when she drove into the side of the Knights of Columbus Hall. Two older ladies heard the noise and came out from the hair salon next door. When seeing the damaged brick wall, and how shaken Summer was, one of the women suggested driver and passenger switch places so it wouldn't hurt the young driver's record. Patti never considered it, not only because she wasn't going to tarnish her driving record but also because it was the right thing to do.

I recently met Lee, a classic car buff, at the 87th birthday party of his Dad, Bruce, one of my card-playing friends. He told about cruising his 1934 Ford down Highway 30 one day that summer. With a top speed of 45 mph, naturally Lee was leading the pack. Behind were another vintage car, a truck and trailer, and five current-day cars, followed by an idiot.

Between Clarence and Lowden, Iowa, there is a straight stretch of several miles in which to safely pass a car. This guy thought he could go around all of them at once without incident. He either didn't see or didn't care about the approaching vehicle he was going to hit head-on.

Realizing the danger they were all in, Lee hit the shoulder, allowing the idiot to move over inches before the crash. This prevented a multiple car pile-up, saving numerous lives.

Steve took driver's education at North Scott High School back when the class was taught during the school day. This was with three students to a car. They were driving down the gravel when they approached a sharp curve in the road. The driver apparently never heard the teacher's screams to slow down. When the dust settled they found themselves sitting in a cornfield.

On Tuesday, Oliver, a current student, witnessed his brother's girlfriend roll her car over on the gravel road in front of his home. She had just bought a late '90s Ford Explorer less than three hours earlier, and was excited to show them her purchase.

When she met Oliver's neighbor's car she tried to move over. Because she was speeding, her car hit the muddy shoulder. Anyone familiar with gravel roads knows that wet ditches suck cars off the road. She overcorrected, causing the SUV to roll over once and back onto its wheels. Unfortunately, the vehicle was totaled. The good news is that she was wearing her seatbelt and not injured, and the Explorer was fully insured.

A few years ago we were driving Highway 136, a dangerous 27- mile stretch from Clinton to Delmar, with a history of many tragic wrecks. Aaron told me his Dad said to be really careful. His uncle had lost six family members in one horrible crash: his parents, two sisters, and two nieces.

Old US Highway 61 is a two-lane road that used to be used by everyone going from Davenport to Dubuque. Before the four-lane was built, thousands of cars used to travel it. The Maquoketa-to Davenport-trip today takes 35 minutes on the four-lane. Thirty years ago it was a 90-minute journey on the two-lane road. On this road south of DeWitt there is a lazy S curve called "Muskrat Curve."

About 30 years ago, a young man I know was going south coming from work. He was distracted and veered into the opposite lane. He met a lady who panicked and crossed over the centerline. When he corrected back into his lane, she died from the head-on collision that resulted. Pay attention, and never drive into the lane of an oncoming car. Take the ditch if you have to.

Another student told of how her grandfather as a young man died on that curve pulling out from his driveway.

An instructor from western Iowa told me that the No. 1 cause of teen fatalities in that part of the state is rollovers on the gravel.

Speed is a factor in almost every crash that there is. If a driver had been driving slower, he probably could have avoided the crash. Depending on the situation, safe may be much slower than the posted speed. The faster you drive, the greater your risk of a crash. The slower you drive, the more time you have to react to any problems you may encounter.

Use a visual search pattern of at least a quarter mile every 12 to 15 seconds. Be alert to changing weather conditions. Watch for hazards, and recognize and obey all road signs. Fifty-four percent of highway fatalities happen on rural roads.[23]

City Driving

Bart is a friend who does most of his teaching in Davenport. He worked with me this past spring in Maquoketa. He loves the rural driving. In the city you are on high alert every second, traveling on many treacherous streets, often with zero-experience drivers. He said we small town instructors get paid way too much for our leisurely outings in the country.

How many mistakes or violations of the law can you count in a two-hour drive? We once ran a contest to do just that. Our student in the back seat was our counter. We had two rules. First, I had to have seen the infraction, and second, we didn't count any perpetrator more than once.

So the lady in Bettendorf was on her phone, didn't signal, never looked, rolled through a stop sign, pulled out in front of us into the wrong lane. We counted her only once. Our winning total in two hours was 123 infractions. Most people had multiple infractions, so the total was probably more than 300.

My brother Mike owns an old miniature motor home. It looks like something an old hippie might drive. A couple of years ago, he was driving with his 4-year-old grandson. Because there is no back seat, Ben was in his booster seat in the right passenger seat.

Mike was pulled over for speeding in a 45 mph zone. The two officers approached the car, one from each side. He apologized and explained he thought that this was a 55 mph zone.

Trying to get out of a fine, he explained that he hadn't had a speeding ticket since the 1970s. The policemen went back to their computer to process the stop.

Meanwhile, Ben said to Grandpa, "Can I ask the man a question?" Mike thought a moment and said, "I'm not sure that would be such a good idea." When the officers returned, Ben rolled down his window and asked, "Do you like doughnuts?" The policeman responded, "I love doughnuts. In fact, I have some in the car with me right now."

Ben looked at the officer. "If you have any with sprinkles, could I have one, please?"

Fortunately, Mike only got a written warning that day.

Nick, one of my students, tells about his sister, Terrible Tonya. She has had six crashes in a year-and-a-half. Four were while she was texting. Tonya graduated early in December, and has been working two jobs to pay for repairs and to maintain her insurance. Nick is bigger than his older sister and doesn't ride with her very often; when he does, she isn't allowed to text.

Here is the list of crashes she has been in: She hit a coyote and wasn't ticketed. Trooper Dan answered that call. She was making a left turn from 53rd Street when a guy traveling at a high rate of speed T-boned her.

Pulling right out of a parking lot, she rear-ended someone waiting at the red light. She ran into the back of Nick's friend's 1987 Camaro in the North High School parking lot. Fortunately for her, that time she sustained all the damage.

She was exiting Interstate 74 onto Interstate 80, a long, winding ramp, when she left the road. On this one, she dented the frame and damaged various other parts underneath the car.

While texting, she damaged her car entering Highway 61 from the Interstate 80 ramp. There is a sign there that says, "Beware of Cross Winds," so she claims it was high winds that blew her off the road. Both Mom and Dad have an app on their cells that lets them check all her calls and texts. They are notified every time she uses her phone.

Nick said his brother is almost as bad. One day on the way to school his brother was tailgating a state trooper on Highway 61. He was trying to get him to move over so he could pass. At the time he was going 71 mph in a 65 mph speed zone.

When he got pulled over, he barely pulled off the pavement. For safety reasons, Nick told his brother he had to move as close to the ditch as possible. The brother asked Nick how he knew that? He said because it was covered in driver's ed class.

It was his lucky day. He only got a warning.

I had one student who claimed his stubborn grandfather had an unusual practice. This guy must have had a lot of time on his hands. Whenever he drove, he never tried to avoid a crash. If he knew the other person was at fault, he would just let them smash into his vehicle. He knew the other party was going to get ticketed and fined. I guess this is an extreme method of showing others that you are right.

I recently finished my third July-August session at Pleasant Valley School. This assignment is top notch. School staff, parents, students are all great to work with. Class is held in a big library with plenty of room for students and me.

The one drawback is driving down 53rd Avenue in Bettendorf. It becomes 53rd Street in Davenport. This may be the busiest street in the Quad-Cities. I take this route eight times most days, sometimes with students having little or no driving experience. At the intersection of Elmore there are nine lanes.

When parents let their child get into a driver education car without practice, they risk the lives of numerous people. A responsible parent gives a teen a chance to have an enjoyable and successful experience. This also helps put them on the path to being a mature and safe driver.

Start your young driver in a big parking lot or a cemetery, then go on to a quiet residential street. As your child's ability improves, increase the difficulty of the drives. As a parent, if you are too afraid, ask the other parent, an aunt, uncle, grandparent or family friend if he or she would be willing to drive with your teen.

Someone recently asked, "What should I do to avoid being tail-gated, and how do I pull over for emergency vehicles on the busy 53rd Street?" I learned at a conference that there are five categories of tailgaters. Some have no intention of passing. Give yourself more following distance. Also, move to the right of your lane, and hope they will go around. If that doesn't work, pull off when you can.

When emergency vehicles approach, pull over to the right if you can. Put your signal on so they will know that you see them. 53rd Street is a busy street with six lanes of traffic. The Elmore intersection has three additional turn lanes. An officer friend says if there is absolutely no way to move to the right, stop on the left. The emergency vehicle will usually be able to cross into the far left lane of the oncoming traffic if it must. He added that most of the time the bottleneck is at the intersection, and motorists oftentimes will turn, which allows police and medical personnel to get through.

Construction Zones

A high school friend, newly 16, ran his car into newly-poured concrete. In 1970, it was an $800 lesson. Today it would cost thousands of dollars to re-pour a batch of cement.

Paris and Sunny were drive partners at North High. Both went by nicknames. They both had difficult names that even their friends struggled with. Paris's Dad was stationed in France when she was born. Sunny must have been the bright spot in her family. Paris was very talkative and had driven a lot. Sunny was inexperienced and more subdued.

We were going east on River Drive through a construction zone. There was no speed posted and Sunny was very nervous. We were traveling too fast for the situation. She hit the curb, flattening the tire and damaging the wheel. Fortunately, we had room to pull off and change the tire.

A friend's sister-in-law is a nurse in Chicago. After work, she was going home to Tinley Park on a Sunday morning at 2 a.m. She thought the speed through construction was 55 mph. There was no work being done at that hour. Only when she got a ticket because a speed-camera caught her going 61 mph in a 45 mph zone did she realize her error. This cost her almost $600.

Thinking she could either reduce or get out of the fine, she went to court. To her dismay more than 200 others were also picked up. After doing the math, I wonder how Illinois can have money problems when they have cameras that print money.

Kevin, a civil engineer, says over 90% of fatalities in work zones are the motorists. We are given plenty of notice that construction is ahead, and nearly all of these crashes are preventable. Most Public Service Announcements and highway signs related to construction are misleading. The messages tell us that speeding fines double in work zones, and it will cost you $10,000 if you hit or kill a construction worker.

Only recently have PSA's started telling us it is the vehicle occupants who usually die at road construction sites.

Distracted drivers don't see traffic slow down ahead. When they do hit their brakes, they don't give the next driver enough time to slow, which sometimes causes a multi-car pile up. Tragically not everyone survives.

If the construction area doesn't have a posted speed, I recommend you go about 10 miles per hour slower than normal. If you slow too much, you increase the odds of being rear-ended.

One-Ways

We primarily drive Dubuque's downtown area for the experience of both city driving and the one-ways. Students have asked if all one-ways were to the left. To some it seemed that way. Learning left turns is the more difficult, so this is where we practice the most.

For years, many of our drivers got confused, as the streets had no pattern. Personally, I believe the architect of these streets had a serious drinking problem!

Ninth, Tenth and Eleventh Streets are east-west streets. They each intersect with Central Avenue, which is a one-way going south. At each of these intersections, the street is a one-way going one direction and a two-way street heading the opposite way. Fortunately for all, the streets department last summer finally fixed the streets in downtown Dubuque. Now there are only two sets of one-ways. Locust and Bluff streets going north and south are at the base of the cliff, and White and Central streets run parallel four or five blocks east and closer to the Mississippi River.

A year ago last spring, Ai, which in Chinese means loving, was turning from 14th Street, a two-way, onto Central, a one-way. She turned into the second lane. When I mentioned the error, she quickly corrected and almost hit a guy flying by us on our left. He probably didn't notice the big STUDENT DRIVER sign on our car. Our passenger observing in the back seat screamed in time for me to hit the dual brake and avoid a crash.

A friend, Sis, grew up driving the flats of Dubuque, the area between the Mississippi River and the bluffs. Some of the people living there refer to themselves as "The Flat's Rats," a little like gym rats, or pool rats. It's actually a term of endearment.

Here's a sideline joke about going one direction when others are not: One afternoon a guy was running some errands for his wife. On his return home, his wife called. She had heard a radio report for all motorists to be cautious. There was some nut driving his pickup truck the wrong direction on the interstate. Concerned, she warned him to be careful if he saw someone driving toward him on the expressway. He said, "What do you mean, one? There are hundreds!"

Do you know the only time you are allowed by law in Iowa to turn left on a red light? Yes, you can turn left on red when you are turning from a one-way onto another one-way.

The purpose of one-ways is to move traffic faster with fewer conflicts. Usually one-ways come in pairs. You will have a street going north and a block over it goes south, or a road is headed westbound and a block over it is going eastbound.

There are several ways of identifying one-ways: An arrow facing one direction, Do Not Enter signs, white lines painted on the street, signs all facing same direction.

Normally cars are all facing the same way. That is everywhere but in Dubuque. Because of the steep hills, many people park facing downhill, regardless what side of the street they are on.

For students who have never driven on one-ways, I teach that you turn into the nearest or closest lane. If the novice can remember that, it will be much less intimidating. Be careful when you follow other drivers, because 50 percent drive into the wrong lane.

We practice right and left turns onto both one-way and two-way streets. This is when students make the most mistakes.

Driving on multi-lane streets does make it more complicated. The best way to learn about one-ways is to practice driving on them.

Parking

Once we were parallel parking in a small town. A young guy who lived in the house came out and said he didn't want us parking behind his car. He had a new model of the cheapest car Chevy made. If he had known how much my employer carries in insurance, he would have hoped we hit his car.

Before Central DeWitt built its new high school, there was always a shortage of parking. Students used to park up to two blocks away on 8th and 10th streets.

One day I drove by and someone did an angle park where the car should have been parallel parked. The back end of the car was sticking out three feet into the street.

I assumed it was a girl. I apologize to the girls for the assumption. The car was a cute little red sedan. If it were a boy, he would have worked until he got it, or would have found a space down the street farther from school. I wish I had taken a picture. Any parent would have gotten pretty excited seeing the rear end of the family car sticking out in traffic that far.

Once in the school parking lot, two Moms crashed. They were dropping their daughters off for class at 7 a.m., and one backed into the other. Can you think of a worse place for that to happen?

To make angle diagonal and perpendicular parking easier, slow down. When you enter the parking space, turn the wheel quickly. Try to avoid parking next to big vehicles. Later, this makes exiting more difficult. When backing, always look over your shoulder, don't use your mirrors.

When leaving, make sure the lane behind you is clear. Back at least half a car length so you don't hit the vehicle next to you; you should turn your wheel quickly. Pull through to the second parking space when possible. It makes exiting much safer when you can drive out rather than back out of a space.

To parallel park, pull alongside the car you want to park behind. Match your back bumper with theirs; then put on your right signal. From here I teach three simple steps. First, crank your wheel all the way to the right, then back to about 30-35 degrees. I tell students when they are half as far as they think they should go, to straighten the wheel, backing until front and back bumpers match. Then crank the steering wheel all the way to the left and ease into the space. Before pulling out, signal and take a good look.

Students are often afraid of parallel parking because of the horror stories they have been told by parents who don't know how to do the procedure. Have you ever noticed how easy some people make it seem? That's because it is.

Normally, people parallel park on busy downtown streets by churches on Sunday mornings. Because we do hundreds each year, we use quiet residential streets. I don't like holding up traffic and it is less stressful for student drivers. Occasionally, people like to watch and see how our students succeed.

School zones

About a year ago, Crystal came and gave a school bus safety presentation for our class. She had received a big ticket after she failed to stop for the flashing red lights of a school bus.

To reduce her fine, she had to create an educational talk and Powerpoint on school bus safety and present it to a driver education class. She was a sophomore and had recently gotten her license.

At a neighboring school a boy also was ticketed for the same offense. He contacted me to present but never followed through. I guess he decided to pay the full fine.

According to a trooper friend, "A child from Iowa has never died in a school bus crash." This is as of the printing of this book.

From town to town, school zone times are not always the same. In Davenport they are different for each school. The high schools, middle schools, and elementary schools run on different schedules. Be aware.

In Iowa, you are required to stop for school buses when the yellow lights come on. They will be turning red soon, and a child will either be getting on or off the bus. If you fail to stop, the fines are almost $700. The exception would be if there are three or more lanes of traffic, or if the bus is on the other side of the median. Bus drivers are not permitted to let children cross more than two lanes.

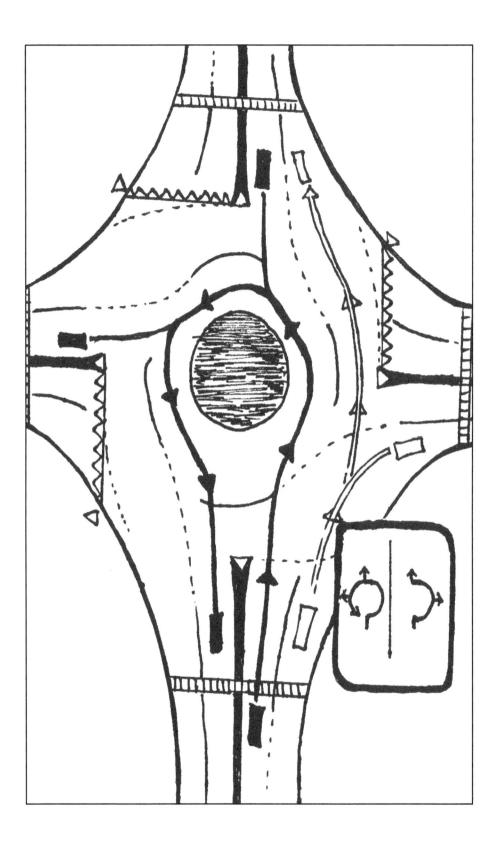

Chapter 7: Red Light, Green Light

Uncontrolled intersections

For nine years, we lived in DeWitt on 5th Street, which had a stop sign at every intersection except 4th Avenue, which was at the end of our block, thus an uncontrolled intersection. A busier street, 4th Avenue, had few stop signs. The result was many crashes, with a lot of ticked-off people.

My neighbor on the corner had small children and was concerned about their safety. He and others had approached the city about putting up a stop sign. They were told that it wasn't in the budget but if the residents bought the signs the city street department would be happy to put them up labor-free. About 10 years later they finally put up stop signs on 5th Street. There must have been enough crashes to warrant the investment.

In Dubuque we drive up Spruce Street, a steep and narrow street. It is only two blocks long and ends at an uncontrolled T-intersection.

To young drivers, it looks impossible to climb and feels as if the car is going to flip over backward. Visibility is poor because the street is lined with parked cars in front of all the old houses, now apartments. Only one car may pass at a time.

At the top we always wait to cross the intersection, even when we are there first. I have never seen anyone stop for us, though the right of way is ours. Upon reaching the peak, we park to switch drivers. One day three of the four drivers hit the curb. I guess this hill shook them more than I realized.

Uncontrolled intersections have no signs or lights indicating who has the right of way. These are generally found in residential neighborhoods. The driver to get to the intersection first gets to go through the intersection first. The second person must yield. If two cars get to an intersection at the same time, the person on the right goes first. It is called "right of way" for a reason, not a "left of way." If two people are coming at each other, the person turning must wait.

If you are on the quieter street coming into an intersection, be careful. The big problem at uncontrolled intersections is that person on the busier street often thinks he has the right of way.

Stop Signs

Parents have concerns as to what kind of driver their teen will be. They will break all the same laws their parents do; for 16 years they have been learning from Mom and Dad.

My brother-in-law got a ticket a couple of years ago for failing to stop for a stop sign. He told the officer he didn't even realize he rolled through. Some people on the road haven't had any driving instruction in decades. Many drivers develop bad habits over time. Others develop poor driving behavior quickly.

Nate had one more hour to complete driver education. Thirty minutes before his final drive he and a friend on mopeds ran a stop sign. They crossed a busy street in front of several cars; our driver education car was second in line.

He got stamped and thus was required to take the drive test at the DOT driving station. Then I wrote a note to his parents explaining that his poor judgment could have resulted in several serious injuries or worse.

A young man didn't see the yellow STUDENT DRIVER sign on the back of our car one day and took out the back end of our driver education car. We had stopped by Kunau Implement, waiting to pull onto Highway 61 heading back to school. Karen was only 15 minutes from completing her six-week, spring driver education class. She was letting our car roll at the stop sign, so I stepped on my teacher brake. In the car behind us, Mitch, 31, was on his phone. He was helping his sister move that day, driving a big Yukon not his own. Our car was totaled. Karen and Latoya, the other driving student, both said they had never heard anyone scream the F-word as loud as when Mitch saw his handiwork.

The deputy said this was the first time in his 17 years he had ever seen a driver education car destroyed. He must have been off duty 10 years earlier when a student rolled the DeWitt driver education car upside down into a creek. More on that story later.

Fortunately, no one was hurt in our crash. My wife, Audrey, picked us up—I lived only a mile from the mishap—and drove us back to school. Using our second driver education car, Karen was able to complete her last drive and receive her certificate of completion that day.

Two months later, Mitch took his case to court. Karen, Deputy Samson, and I each had to drive to Clinton to testify as witnesses. I felt bad for Karen. She was a 17-year-old high school senior who had to scrape together gas money to make the 70-mile round trip.

I assume Mitch was trying to save his license. He had no attorney and didn't exude much confidence. In fact, he looked as though he'd just been beaten with a club.

Mitch's fines and related costs must have been considerable. But what can be more embarrassing than explaining to your buddies how you totaled a car with a big STUDENT DRIVER sign on it because you didn't see it.

Adam, now in his early 70s, was a farm kid from rural Bettendorf who had started driving at 9 years old. His driving instructor was a gravelly-voiced man who was also the head football coach. He asked, "Who has driving experience?" Adam responded that he had. Later, his teacher almost put everyone through the windshield when Adam failed to stop for the temporary sign in front of a school. This was a humbling experience for Adam, a kid who had been driving in the fields and on the gravel for years. Maybe the teacher should have asked if anyone had experience driving in town?

Because Hattie's brother has twice rear-ended people at stop signs, his insurance is high. He doesn't pay attention and assumes everyone else also has the bad habit of rolling through stop signs.

A trooper friend tells a mythical story that makes a great point. One day he and his partner stopped a young man for rolling through a stop sign. This guy had a bad attitude and a smart mouth. "What difference does it really make, I slowed down," he snarled.

The other officer pulled out his night stick and started smacking the kid on the head. Pretty soon the crybaby started shouting, "STOP, STOP." My friend asked, "Do you want him to slow down or stop? There is a difference. "

He tells about a neighbor's son who was killed. The man was thrown from the car not wearing a seat belt. If the officer had been a little more observant, he might have given this guy a ticket at some point and he might still be alive today.

I had my chiropractor appointment in Park View one morning. I was coming home and two miles south of DeWitt someone ran the stop sign and pulled in front of me. As we approached town at Highway 30, a semi pulled in front of both of us coming off the ramp. Fifty yards farther another semi ran the stop sign, pulling in front of him.

Then at the BP station, 100 yards to the north, a third semi pulled in front of all four of us. Lots of examples of rolling through stop signs!

The first stop sign was used in 1915 in Detroit, Mich. It was white with black letters. In 1922 the octagon sign was first proposed to make it unique. In 1954 the stop sign became red with white lettering.[24]

Half of all vehicle crashes occur at intersections.[25] A trooper friend shared that 70% of all stops at stop signs are illegal and they are called a roll-through. Several people have told me they thought seven out of 10 was too low an estimate. Stop behind the white stop line. If there is no stop line, then stop behind the crosswalk. When there is neither, stop behind the sidewalk. At times there is nothing but the stop sign. Then you should make a complete stop before the intersection. I usually tell students to stop halfway between the sign and the intersecting street. The reason is that in rural areas, the stop sign may be yards from the intersection, with poor visibility.

You have made a complete stop when your body settles back in the seat. Look both ways at least twice before proceeding through. That second look will help you see traffic, which is sometimes obscured by the front post next to your windshield, a blind spot.

When you are stopped at a blind intersection where you can't see traffic because of a bush, tree, fence, sign, parked car, snow piles, etc., make sure you completely stop then creep forward until you see if it is safe to go.

Traffic lights

Recently we were driving west on 53rd Street in Bettendorf. The eastbound traffic had a green light for people going straight and those making a left turn. We stopped for our red light. Amanda, my student driver, was pretty inexperienced. When our light turned green, she hesitated much longer than was normal. Then a person running the red light turned left in front of us four seconds after the light had gone red. My students and I could have been T-boned. I applaud the red light cameras. The number of people in Davenport and Bettendorf who run red lights continues to amaze me.

When my daughter Whitney moved from Phoenix to Milwaukee, her insurance rates went down by two-thirds. Her deductible was cut in half and she had double the coverage. She had a friend she worked with in Arizona who had five major crashes, none of them her fault.

Whitney became anxious to move back to the Midwest after almost being killed. She was making a left turn at a green light.

She was in the intersection, as we teach, waiting for all the oncoming traffic to get through. Otherwise you could wait all day at a busy intersection. By the time it was her turn, the light was already red. She almost got through her left turn when a lady coming at her ran the red light at 50 mph, hitting her back bumper. If she had been a second sooner, she would have T-boned Whitney and killed her.

Lee and Josh are former students. Once their Mom was driving in Chicago's city traffic and was pretty intimidated. She was afraid to pull into the intersection to make a left turn. Each time the light turned yellow, cars were still coming from the other direction.

The traffic was so heavy there was never going to be an opportunity to turn. Josh said his mother waited for a half hour. It was probably a couple of cycles of the light, which seemed like 30 minutes. Finally, the police officer in the car behind knocked on her window. "Lady, you have to pull forward or we all will spend the entire day at this intersection."

Don, another Davenport driving instructor, and his students were driving south on Marquette Street. At Kimberly Road, a woman, 87, ran the red light. She hit the front right panel of the driver education car. If they had been hit a half-second later, Don would have died in a T-bone collision that day.

The student driver was a senior at Central High. He was a football player and track athlete, a very good driver who kept his calm better than either his teacher or drive partner.

The lady kept saying her chest hurt. She was taken to the hospital and released, they thought with no serious injuries. Unfortunately, she died two weeks later.

Some western Iowa teachers drive with three students in the car, because it takes an hour to get to a traffic light where students can practice in city traffic.

Controlled intersections are those with traffic lights, stop signs, or yield signs. In 1924 the first traffic light used was made by the Acme Company.[26] In city driving, many crashes occur at traffic lights. Be aware, some people run red lights.

Roundabouts

Everyone is supposed to go right. This spring and summer my son-in-law in Mount Vernon, Iowa, saw two different people going left on the newly constructed roundabout, creating a lot of stress for everyone they met. What confuses new users is the arrow for people going to the left or straight and the tire tracks all over the concrete in the center.

This summer we were driving the two roundabouts by Mount Vernon, Iowa. We were coming from the west on the east roundabout. Coming off there are two lanes. My student driver hesitated only for a moment, and a guy passed us going over the center hump. Why was this person in such a hurry? Did he not see the STUDENT DRIVER sign? He endangered the safety of several people and could have caused thousands of dollars in damages. Plus, that would have been a $195 fine. I have been back to that site several more times and wonder how he was able to get by us.

If you have never seen a roundabout before, even with the speed as slow as 15 mph the experience can be pretty confusing. It doesn't help when drivers don't yield as they are supposed to, either. I have had students actually drive up the hump and onto the decorative red bricks in the middle. There will be more and more roundabouts built, so drivers need to learn how to maneuver through them.

The big selling point of roundabouts is they eliminate head-on collisions and T-bones, which kill many people each year. Not having to sit at a red light also eliminates burning extra time and gasoline.

For semi drivers and people pulling trailers, they can be quite challenging, though. That is why you sometimes see tire marks across the center island.

They have been using them in Europe for probably 50 years. How could they not be a good idea?

Railroads

We were once at the railroad crossing in Mechanicsville. When people leave town they have to cross the tracks right next to Highway 30. There is room for only two cars between the stop sign and the tracks. The lady ahead of us was vehicle No. 3 when a train approached. She had about 10 seconds to react to the flashing red lights and the descending gate. She pulled into the left lane. I guess if you live in a town where frequent trains a day come through, this probably occurs regularly.

The same trains go through DeWitt. The southbound traffic has two gates before the tracks in DeWitt. One is for the dead track on the north, which is no longer used. The lights went on and I didn't know how much time we had. Our driver was very inexperienced and I wasn't about to take a chance crossing.

I stopped our car, not knowing there was a second gate until we were struck by it. We now found ourselves between the two descended gates with newly acquired scratches on the trunk of our vehicle. It was embarrassing sitting there as the train rolled by.

One night my younger brother was out with a friend. They were both college age. Dean had borrowed his Dad's new Lincoln for the evening. They had been barhopping. It was after midnight and they were headed to the Golden Toad, a bar owned by two of my brothers. On the way, they approached a railroad crossing with multiple tracks.

The story he told 35 years ago was that the train's light wasn't working. Not seeing anything, they innocently drove around the gate to cross the tracks. They almost succeeded when the train struck the car's back axle. They were dragged a block before the car came free.

No one was hurt, but they had to go to the hospital. The wait was quite lengthy because the personnel were gearing up for the railroad accident victims. Eventually, when the staff learned they were the crash victims, they were attended to and then allowed to go home. Recently I learned that the train's headlight and gate had been operational. The real reason Dean drove around the gate at the railroad tracks was that his judgment was impaired by the alcohol he had drunk.

He was knocked out when his head hit either the steering wheel or the windshield. The trip to the hospital was necessary to attend to the injured Dean.

My brother was uninjured, so this gave him plenty of time to fabricate a story to tell both sets of parents. For a long time afterward, he was pretty nervous every time he approached a railroad crossing. With us, once in the fog, he actually got out of the car to look both ways, then walked across the tracks before getting back into the car.

Cy shared the story about his Grandma Camp. At the time, she was a young city girl newly married to a farmer and living near the railroad tracks.

One night she was awakened by a train's whistle. At the window she eyed the speedy locomotive, and to her horror a half-mile up the track she spotted a second charging train coming from the opposite direction. Frantically, she shook her husband awake to also witness this head-on collision.

Fortunately there was no loss of life or any damage done when the two trains harmlessly passed each other on parallel tracks.

One of my college classmates, nicknamed Buford, was a hippie with long, blond stringy hair and rimless glasses, who couldn't grow a beard. He lasted only one year, but before he left, Buford shared this story.

There was an abandoned railroad track near his rural home. He claimed his Dad's old pickup's wheels had the same width as the rails. He and his friends would put the truck on the tracks and let some air out of the tires. Then they would let it drive in low gear with a brick on the gas pedal, while they sat in the back drinking beer.

I have been told that 85 trains go through DeWitt every 24 hours. Unfortunately, people do die in our community from train crashes. You can never be too vigilant.

Chapter 8: Sharing the Road
When You Don't Want To

Bicycles

A year-and-a-half ago I read about a guy in Florida who rides 25 miles to work each day. Motorized vehicles have crashed into him three times. Most recently he was hit by a black bear. Obviously, his route isn't the safest. How much longer is he going to challenge fate?

RAGBRAI is one of the most enjoyable, satisfying, and out-of-the-ordinary experiences I have ever been a part of. RAGBRAI, The Des Moines Register's Annual Great Bike Ride Across Iowa, is a weeklong trip across Iowa in July, with more than 20,000 cyclists. People from every state and many countries make this annual trek. It is the oldest, longest, and biggest bike ride in the world.

It starts on Sunday in western Iowa. The tradition is for participants to dip their back tire into the Missouri River. The following Saturday the bike ride ends in eastern Iowa, where riders dip their front tire in the Mississippi River. Each rider who completes all seven days will have pedaled 350-400 miles.

RAGBRAI provides experiences each rooky could never have anticipated. These include excitement, fun, work, pain, fear, struggle, challenge, companionship, confidence, sound sleep, good food, weight loss, and actualization.

The route is different each summer. Iowans hope it comes through their town every four or five years. It is a boon and great recognition for small communities across the state. In each town the locals lay out the red carpet. They provide free entertainment, bicycle repair, beer tents, and great food at reasonable prices.

In the host cities, where the riders stay overnight, they provide even more amenities. These include church services, a free swim, shuttles, showers, and campsites at parks, school properties, or acres of empty fields.

Some rise early and complete the day's ride before breakfast. Others stop and enjoy what each town offers. Some partiers start at midday, after sleeping off last night's drunk.

For a principal friend of mine, and thousands more, this is their family holiday each summer. When anyone marries into Mick's family, he or she is taken out to buy a bicycle, with instructions to start training.

For five summers I rode a bike about a thousand miles a season. My routes had good visibility and minimal traffic. Bright clothing and a flashing red light were always a must. I frequently rode to places like Clinton, in and around DeWitt, Lost Nation, Donahue, and Olin, confident I would return home safely from each ride. During this time I rode one or two days of RAGBRAI each July. On one of these rides I was riding by myself, so I had all my gear packed on my bike. When I entered the edge of Ankeny, an overnight stop that year, people were greeting and cheering on the riders at the end of their long day.

I stopped and asked one woman where I could camp overnight. She introduced herself as Mary, a local nurse practitioner. "I live five houses down, you can pitch your tent in our yard," she said. When I got all settled she introduced me to Stan, her husband, the high school band director. They invited me in to show me where the shower and the towels were. Next, she said they were going to be gone for a couple of hours checking out all the festivities downtown. "Here is the TV remote, feel free to watch television while we are gone."

The next morning they fed me a full breakfast and shared a delightful hour of conversation.

During the night my bike tire went soft. Stan took me down to a bike station to get it repaired. This trip took an hour.

When I finally got my bike all packed up and was leaving, they wished me well. Where else but in Iowa, would people invite a total stranger into their home while they were gone.

Two summers in a row I rode 200 miles from my home to Kenosha, Wis., my parent's farm. I traveled across northern Illinois, staying the first night in Mt. Morris with the second in Janesville, Wis., with family. I arrived at Mom and Dad's by noon on the third day. On my first trek, I was oblivious to the dangers, because I was so excited about accomplishing my goal.

The next year before my trip to Kenosha, I rode two days of RAGBRAI, then on to the farm. This ride was 340 miles in four-and-a-half days. Drivers committed assorted traffic violations putting me in peril. They ran stop signs, passed on yellow lines, and even passed on narrow roads while meeting oncoming traffic.

One maniac went around me, forcing an oncoming semi into the ditch. People from Iowa and Wisconsin have nasty names for this type of Illinois driver. They call them IBs for Illinois Bas-----. Some are even less charitable and call them FIBs. I'm pretty sure others from their state think of them the same way we do.

I could have been killed a dozen times on that second trip across northern Illinois. Arriving safely at the farm, I vowed I would never make that ride again. My passion for biking pretty much died. It was two years before I shared with Audrey the numerous scares I really had.

Guy, a bicycle shop owner, told me that once a rider sustains serious injuries, he or she never has the same enthusiasm for cycling again. Sounds very similar to my experience, except I didn't have to get hurt.

Occasionally, I train and compete in a swim meet, road race, or adventure race of canoeing, biking, and jogging. At my age, if you are able to finish, you usually get a medal. These events for the most part satisfy my competitive urges.

I still take spin classes and ride my recumbent exercise bike 100 miles every week. I have had the same bike for 12 years and have logged more than 30,000 miles. If I fall off, I won't sustain any broken bones or major road rash.

My brother once broke his collarbone while riding. A friend broke both collarbone and a wrist. Guy told me that when you take a spill, tuck your shoulder and roll. This will prevent these two injuries.

Chuck, a retired police chief, crashed on RAGBRAI. Yes, some injuries do occur. Riders really need to be careful everywhere they ride. His narrow front tire hit a crack in the pavement. He was propelled like a pebble from a slingshot. Chuck's head hit the pavement; his helmet was mashed but saved his life. He spent a night in the hospital with bleeding on the brain. He lost his ability to read, which eventually came back with five months of intense therapy.

My son Tyler doesn't like bicycles. He drove construction equipment for four-and-a-half years, and a delivery truck two years in Austin, Texas. He has had to avoid hundreds of potential crashes with bike riders violating numerous laws. Austin is the home of a famous, now dethroned Tour De France champion. Down there the cyclist is king. If you hurt a cyclist, you're going to prison.

One beautiful Saturday in April my son-in-law's former coworker and two friends were hit while riding. A lady concentrating on her CD-player ran over them. Each sustained life-altering injuries including a broken back, broken neck, and a serious concussion. This happened in Mesa, Ariz., the day before Easter.

A local teacher was hit the first week of school last August riding his bike home from school. He spent weeks in the hospital and is fortunate to be alive today.

The "Running Machine" was invented in 1817. With two wheels it looked like today's bike. It was propelled like the Fred Flintstone car, with your feet.

The velocipede, or bone shaker, was invented in the 1860s. This was built with a wood frame and metal tires. It was propelled with pedals on the front wheel and was very uncomfortable to ride.

In the 1870s, the high wheel bicycle, the first vehicle to be called a bicycle, was introduced. These had a metal frame, rubber wheels, and were much more comfortable to ride.

The Rover Safety bicycle was invented in 1885. These had a metal chain with two same-sized wheels. John Boyd Dunlop developed the air-filled tire in 1888, which created a smoother ride. In the 1920s, children's bikes were introduced. Racing bikes became popular in the 1960s, with mountain bikes to follow in the 1980s.[27] Worldwide, bicycles are the No. 1 source of transportation. Bicycles by law are considered vehicles. Riders have the same rights and responsibilities as those driving motorized vehicles. Two percent of all roadway fatalities are bicyclists. Nine percent of those are age 14 and younger, 69% are boys.[28] In 2012, 726 bicyclists died in crashes. Another 49,000 were injured; 88% killed and 80% injured were males. Forty-three was the average age of those who died while biking.[29]

Don't honk at bicyclists; you may startle them. Give bikes plenty of room when passing, in case they swerve to miss a road hazard. Beware, children often pull out in front of traffic. Bicyclists often don't stop for stop signs. Stop signs slow them down too much and require more effort to restart.

A bicyclist should always wear a helmet. Obey all traffic laws. Always stay in the right lane unless you're turning left. Never ride against traffic. If you ride at night use headlight, taillights, reflectors, and wear easily visible clothing.

Public service announcements on radio and television recommend people ride their bikes to work. If your route includes heavily traveled streets and highways, this would in my opinion be a big mistake. There are just too many stressed, fatigued, and distracted drivers for you to be safe. Add to the mix a hand full of crazies behind the wheel. I applaud the millions who ride for their exercise. That is, if they ride in safe locations.

Motorcycles

Marcus was 200 pounds and had a 125cc Harley. When we were kids, he used to do a half-a-mile-long wheelie on his dead-end road. He and Parker, another friend, used to jump the creek on our farm with their bikes. It had to be 30 feet across.

Once when we were camping in our woods, we kept the neighbors awake while we raced through the straw stubble much of the night. Dad never allowed that to happen again.

We live along Highway 61, a four-lane expressway. For two summers we had a bright yellow crotch rocket doing a wheelie at 70 mph going by our place, for more than two miles. He was up when he came into view, and still on one wheel going out of sight. We haven't seen him in a while. I wonder if he is still alive.

My brother Mark and I owned a 350 Honda, back when we were in college. In the '70s, I believe this was the most popular bike on the road. When Audrey and I were dating, we would ride it occasionally the 60 miles from her family's farm in Janesville to my family's farm by Kenosha. Any time you drove more than 20 miles, the vibration would really make your bottom hurt. Audrey was always trying to get me to stop and rest. Always in a hurry, I responded with, "The pain isn't going to get any worse. Let's just keep going."

A couple of weeks one summer I drove to West Bend, Wis., 70 miles each way to work. I had to leave each morning at 4:30 to start at 6 a.m. Living by Lake Michigan, the challenge was wearing enough clothes to stay warm in the morning. The dew was heavy and I would arrive at work soaked. At the end of the day, packing everything on the bike when leaving for home was a challenge, as I didn't have luggage racks or saddle bags.

My wife, Audrey, recently saw a guy texting while riding his motorcycle. He had no helmet. I have seen someone ride a bike in city traffic doing the same thing.

My nephew owned a bike, and at one of the family picnics he let his novice cousin ride. They were both university students. She accidentally cranked the throttle, lost control and crashed. This happened on Sunday. She went to the hospital with a splitting headache. They sent her home. It wasn't discovered until Tuesday that she had a broken neck.

My son, Tyler, said he is afraid of motorcycles. His best friend is in the cycle business; he doesn't ride for the same reason.

Logan, as a young man just out of the service, had a crash. It was not his fault. He instantly realized the dangers, and never rode his motorcycle again.

In this latest driver's ed session, I had a student whose Dad used to race motorcycles. When he got married and started his family, he weighed the dangers and quit riding altogether.

Several years later this man's father was in a serious cycle crash and lived the last few years of his life as a paraplegic.

Kirk, a friend, was on his way to school one morning on Highway 61. He was passed by a blur. Up the road two miles, that same motorcycle and its rider were lying in the ditch. On the road were deer parts everywhere. At between 90-100 mph, the animal disintegrated upon impact. According to the paper, the cyclist, wearing a helmet, suffered only two broken wrists. In this case his speed might be what saved his life.

I recently saw a guy puffing on his cigarette while skateboarding down the street.

Fortunately, we don't see Ape Hangers much anymore. These are big, high motorcycle handlebars that make it more difficult to steer and balance. How could riding down the highway doing pull-ups be comfortable or safe?

I also wonder why they make cycles go so fast? If you ride them at 194 mph, the speed they are capable of going, you will die.[30]

A couple of years ago, Darcy, a friend, and his wife were on vacation at a campground down South. At a stop sign, they passed another motorcyclist, who waved. After the biker pulled out, he passed Darcy and a car. Up the road a bit, a motorist thought he could beat the line of traffic. He never saw the motorcycle. Upon impact the rider flew a distance and landed in the field. He was wearing a helmet. I hope he survived.

I know of several people who had good friends lost while out riding. Soon after my father was drafted into World War II, he lost his best friend in a motorcycle accident.

Kevin, a teacher friend, tells the story of his buddy in college. He asked him if he would give him a ride back to school after he dropped his bike off. Kevin followed and the guy took off like the wind, lost control and hit a telephone pole. He wasn't wearing a helmet. Kevin was the first on the scene. He never again wants to relive that nightmare. When his children became of age, none were allowed to own a cycle.

One of my fellow driving instructors lost his college roommate. One day he was out for a ride and he never came home.

The following are statistics from Iowa, one of the few states that does not require helmet use while operating a motorcycle. Sixty percent of riders killed were 45 or older. Nine out of 10 victims were not wearing helmets.[30]

One in two fatal motorcycle crashes involved no other vehicles. Speed is reported as a contributing factor in more than one-third of Iowa's fatal motorcycle crashes. Over one third of motorcycle operators in fatal collisions tested positive for alcohol or drugs.

More than 50 percent of motorcycle-vehicle crashes occurred because a driver did not see the motorcycle. Left-turning motorists and drivers at stop signs often "misjudge speed" or "don't see" an approaching motorcycle.[31]

There is a motorcycle education group that gives safety talks to driver's education classes. I will not have them in my class because they don't advocate the use of helmets. Per vehicle miles traveled, motorcyclists are about 30 times more likely than passenger car occupants to die in a traffic crash, according to the National Highway Traffic Safety Administration NHTSA.[32]

Why wouldn't you do everything you can to try to protect riders? It seems this group wants everyone else to be responsible for the well being of the motorcyclist except for the riders themselves.

Darcy said he would never belong to this group. He believes they are not being accountable when they don't recommend helmet use.

Semis

Sam, a trucker, hauls cattle to the Iowa State Fair in Des Moines every August for the local FFA students from Cedar County. When his cattle are unloaded he usually stops and has a cup of coffee with Russ, the head of transportation.

On this last trip to Des Moines, the traffic was bottlenecked at the entrance to the fairgrounds. Sam was unable to get far enough to the left, which was required to make a safe right turn. He politely asked the guy with the flashlight to please have the barricades moved.

Flashlight Guy, enjoying his power, hollered for Sam to get his truck out of the way and then slammed the cab door in Sam's face. Sam did as he was told, running over one gate with his tractor and the other with his trailer.

"My boss is going to have you arrested for damaging fair property," Flashlight Guy exclaimed.

Sam said, "Go get Russ. I would like to speak with him."

"Do you know my supervisor?"

"Yes, we have been friends for years," Sam said. The crowd of gathering workers really enjoyed this conversation.

Flashlight Guy, now very polite, instructed Sam to go and unload, and he would take care of moving the barriers.

Sid, an old friend, drove semi for over 25 years. About 10 years ago he had two bad crashes in six months. No one died, but in both crashes people were hurt severely. For the next year he had recurring nightmares of an old couple in their torn-apart motor home careening down the interstate. Sid no longer drives.

He was forced to choose another career so he could sleep at night.

Many of America's goods are transported by tractor-trailers. Most people call them semis. These trucks are made of steel, are big, heavy, and require long stopping distance.

Always give these trucks plenty of space. They are unable to stop quickly and require lots of room to make safe turns, both to the left and right. It is hard for them to maintain a consistent speed on hills, where they require more time accelerating and stopping. When they carry heavy loads, they are even more dangerous.

Semis have four no-zone blind spots where they are unable to see other vehicles. These are the areas by the front bumper on both left and right sides, and behind to the right and left corners. Respect them. It is very risky to drive in their no zones, tailgate them, or cut them off.

Pedestrians

Karl, our neighbor, had younger siblings, but none close to our age, so growing up he practically lived at our farm. Halloween was always a big event for us. For little kids, it meant some independence and lots of candy. Easter was the only other day of the year that we were allowed unlimited sweets.

Did you know that a 10-year-old boy has a brain. Two 10-year-olds have half a brain between them. Three or more have no brains at all.

By the time we were 10 or 11, Karl and I and my brother were on our own. No more car rides for us. That night Karl came well equipped for trick or treating. He had a giant white shopping bag along with a monster flashlight, the kind policemen used to carry, that held at least 10 D batteries. After leaving Karl's house, we cut through his next-door neighbor's lifeless garden. Noticing the dead tomatoes, Karl and I decided these might be useful.

After mine leaked all over my hands, I discarded them. We had only gotten about a quarter mile when someone came cruising down this quiet road. Splat, then we heard screeching brakes. When the car backed up, we were off to the races. My brother was late at the start because he didn't know about the tomatoes. Even at that young age, he and I were athletic. We slipped through the barbed wire then hid in the hayfield. Karl got stuck in the fence with his beacon shining on his candy bag. It glowed brighter than a billboard advertisement.

Two angry young men soon captured Karl. Repeatedly he begged, "Please don't kill me. Please don't kill me." Then he claimed it was his friends' fault. The hunt began for the two of us. When my brother was discovered, one guy said to his friend, "Look, I got me one."

Determining that Karl actually was the culprit, they made him remove his shirt and clean the window, all the while threatening his life if he ever did anything so stupid again.

I listened to all of this from my hiding place deeper in the field. After being released unharmed, Karl was fortunate my brother didn't wallop him. This was just the first of our many Oct. 31 adventures.

I saw one guy walking down the sidewalk with the top of his pants below the bottom of his boxers. My niece's husband, a cop, really doesn't mind these people. He says, "They are a gift from God." When they are pursued, they can't run very well and are easy to apprehend.

Tony used to sometimes see double when drinking. He was a good high school friend who later attended UW-Madison. It was a good thing his choice of transportation was an old bike most of the five years he went to the University. No one ever stole primitive two-wheelers. Besides, whenever he saw double he would cover one eye so he could better make his way. This was either walking or cycling.

All users of roadways and parking lots should be respectful of others who share these areas. Would it kill pedestrians to wait five seconds to let a vehicle pass? It might save their life. When visiting Ty and his family in Texas, I always get a surprised look when I, as a pedestrian, wait and don't make drivers stop for me.

Seniors

The following is reprinted with permission from "The Gift of Attitude" by Sam Glenn, about an 88-year-old woman.

Dear Granddaughter,

The other day I went up to our local Christian bookstore and saw a "Honk if You Love Jesus" bumper sticker. I was feeling particularly sassy that day because I had just come from a thrilling choir performance followed by a thunderous prayer meeting. So I bought the sticker and put it on my bumper.

Boy, am I glad I did! What an uplifting experience that followed. I was stopped at a red light at a busy intersection, just lost in thought about the Lord and how good he is, and I didn't notice that the light had changed.

It is a good thing someone else loves Jesus because if he hadn't honked, I'd never have noticed. I found that lots of people love Jesus! While I was sitting there, the guy behind started honking like crazy, and then he leaned out of his window and screamed, "For the love of God! Go! Go! Go! Jesus Christ, Go!"

What an exuberant cheerleader he was for Jesus!

Everyone started honking! I just leaned out my window and started waving and smiling at all those loving people. I even honked my horn a few times to share in the love!

There must have been a man from Florida back there, because I heard him yelling something about a sunny beach.

I saw another guy waving in a funny way with only his middle finger stuck up in the air. I asked my young teenage grandson in the back seat what that meant.

He said it was probably a Hawaiian good luck sign or something. Well, I have never met anyone from Hawaii, so I leaned out the window and gave him the good luck sign right back.

My grandson burst out laughing. Why, even he was enjoying this religious experience!!

A couple of the people were so caught up in the joy of the moment that they got out of their cars and started walking towards me. I bet they wanted to pray or ask what church I attended, but this is when I noticed the light had changed. So, grinning, I waved at all my brothers and sisters, and drove on through the intersection.

I noticed that I was the only car that got through the intersection before the light changed again, and felt kind of sad that I had to leave them after all the love we had shared. So I slowed the car down, leaned out the window, and gave them all the Hawaiian good luck sign one last time as I drove away. Praise the Lord for such wonderful folks!!

Will write again soon.

Love,

Granny

We had a friend who should not have been driving. His wife, for health reasons, was no longer able to. Now in his early 80s this was the one thing he believed he was still able to do. We didn't know how bad his driving was until his wife died. Only then did we realize she had been helping him find his way to the bank each week. He had been doing business there for decades. No one knew how long this had gone on.

Our family doctor has lost patients when he informed them they shouldn't be driving anymore. He said a friend who is a surgeon says it is easier to tell patients they have cancer than to tell them they should stop driving. Still, let the professionals break the news to them.

Eugene, a friend, is 93. He drives everywhere, as well as at night. You would never guess he was over 80. He held a job till age 79, and now works out six days a week. He has a spring in his step with a positive attitude of someone half his age.

Before I gave my driving talk "Come Drive With Me: The Adventures, Perils, and Insights of a Driving Instructor" at The Saint Sebastian's senior group, feisty, 88-year-old Jean, my Mom's Scrabble buddy, asked if I knew what a fog line was? I told her no. We were about to begin my talk, so she was going to finish the story when I was done. Afterward, she related another story and forgot all about the fog line.

I later asked a couple of instructor friends. They didn't know. It wasn't in the driver education book either. I asked a trooper friend; he knew. It must be something they teach at the police academy. The fog line is the white line on the left and right edges of the road.

I had to call my mother to get the rest of the story from Jean. One day Jean was pulled over while driving down the highway. The police officer following noticed she was weaving in her lane. He pulled her over and inquired whether she had been drinking.

"No, I have not," was her reply. The officer asked, "Then why do you keep weaving onto the shoulder? That's not safe or legal."

"Every time I meet a truck that is on the center line, I am going to continue to drive on the fog line so I don't get smashed," she replied. He told her she wasn't going to get hit by a semi. He must have liked her spunk because she didn't get a ticket. Looking back, she said she wished he had requested a field sobriety test, just for the experience of it and to tell her friends.

At that same talk, my then 91-year-old mother, for a laugh, asked who taught my 10 siblings and me how to drive? I acknowledged that she had. I think her lifelong courage is what gives her longevity and she got a hearty applause.

I grew up in the '50s and '60s. Both my grandfathers had died and neither of my grandmothers ever drove.

In Wisconsin, my father in 1934 at age 16 sent 25 cents to Madison, the state capital. He became a legal driver when he received his cloth license in the mail. At 90, they issued him his new license. It is valid until age 98. He said to my wife, Audrey, "Can you believe they would do that?"

Dad, 97, and Mom, 93, are still pretty good drivers. Someone always gives them a ride to family get-togethers and the many funerals they attend. They only drive to church, the library, to Scrabble, Sheepshead games, and the few stores they shop at— just during the day and on less traveled roads.

A couple of years ago they got in big trouble for being out until 9:30 p.m. They are free all day. Why do they have to be out after dark? They also get scolded if they drive in bad weather.

Each Christmas and Easter, Mom creates beautiful painted cards then has a hundred copies professionally printed. In December 2013, my parents went to South Milwaukee to pick up the work when it was complete.

A six-inch snowstorm hit sooner than was expected, and a 30-minute trip home took 90. When they finally arrived back at the farm, my two brothers wanted to know, "Where the h--- have you been?" With 11 children and 33 grandchildren to watch their every move it can be h---. It is like being in high school all over again with curfews and restricted driving.

Now whenever snow is forecast, my brother parks his big equipment behind their car in the shop. Mom says, "They don't think I should still be driving, but it is still okay for me to make apple pies for all the family functions and paint 400 Christmas cookies each holiday season."

Lee and Josh's grandfather used to drive from his home in Clinton to visit the kids in Maquoketa. According to the boys, Grandpa had a lot of time and was always trying to get the best gas mileage on his trips. He was once pulled over on Highway 30 going 35 or 40 in a 65 mph zone. He was cited for going too slow. He called his son, a lawyer in Clinton, to see if he could fix his ticket. He was disappointed when Junior said, "Pay the ticket, because you're a hazard on the road."

Stan, a Twin Cites native, related the story of his childhood friend. After this event, Linda knew for sure her Dad's driving days were over.

One day she received an accidental call from her Mom's cell phone. It must have been a butt dial. Dad and Mom, now in their 80s, were out running an errand and unaware their conversation was being listened to by their middle-aged daughter.

Here is how the conversation went: Dad said to Mom, "I can't find the brake." She responded with, "I told you it is the pedal on the left, the one I put the orange tape on, so you could see it."

With Linda's testimonial, the family's doctor informed Dad he was no longer going to be allowed to drive on streets and highways.

If you have a parent or grandparent still driving, whose safety you are concerned about, have your Doctor talk to them. They are more likely to accept the inevitable from a professional, but not always, than from the person whose diapers they once changed.

Young drivers are anxious to get their license and freedom. Seniors are trying to keep their license and freedom. Here are a few strategies that can help older people drive safely as long as possible.

For seniors, planning is important when they drive. Things to consider include being well rested with a properly maintained vehicle. Windows and lights should be cleaned off, with mirrors set properly.

Eliminate distractions such as GPS, music, and pets. If you feel stressed, avoid busy roads or highways, and driving at night. Often older drivers have depth perception problems. Many of their crashes occur while making left turns.

Map your route before you leave home; try to avoid left turns unless you have a dedicated left turn arrow.

Don't drive more than 10 mph under the speed limit. This dramatically increases the odds of being rear-ended.

In parking lots, drive through to the second space and park, so when you leave you can pull out, which is safer than backing out.

Everyone is different. Some seniors are able to safely drive well into their 90s, while others are no longer safe in their 60s or 70s.

Chapter 9: Adverse Conditions
"There are no Vacation Emergencies"

Fog

In December, we were driving to Maquoketa in the fog. Visibility was poor. A guy passed us going 75 mph while texting. We couldn't believe this and hoped he got to where he needed to be safely.

Fog delays are common for schools in eastern Iowa. Most are two-hour delays in starting the school day. Usually the fog lifts and all goes back to normal. When the weather doesn't improve, this is when it is the most dangerous for children. Drivers aren't expecting to see a bus on its route during mid-morning.

We live on Old Highway 61. It is the frontage road to the new four-lane. When the fog is bad we can't even see our house or the lights on the property. The fog is so disorienting; with no landmarks it is easy to make a wrong turn. More than once I turned north on the highway rather than onto our little road.

We have lived in our home in the country for 25 years. It is an old farmhouse with many recent improvements. Shortly after our move we added Abby, a sheltie-cross puppy, to our family. She was a great watchdog, alerting us to all activity outside. A smart and quick dog that used to catch birds from the air, and kill rats that came near our pumpkin crop.

A single mother lived in the house for six months before us. She was an illegal drug dealer, with a live-in local petty criminal. After this perpetrator assaulted her and threatened to kill her, she made a hasty departure.

Two weeks later on a foggy night this guy was out with a fellow felon robbing homes, when they ran out of gas. While they were attempting to hitch a ride to get fuel on Highway 61 north of Maquoketa, the companion was hit and killed by a truck.

Our dog Abby was a fearful dog, but loved almost everyone. We had a neighbor before Roy who must have done something to her, because she never gave him a pleasant reception.

For the first couple of years, strangers would stop occasionally looking for their dealer or her guy. Abby could either sense they were bad people or she could smell the drugs. She would go crazy and each time you thought she was going to tear them apart.

Two people who had major influence in my life hit and killed people in the fog. Neither was at fault.

The first was one of my high school coaches. He was one of the people who encouraged me to follow my dreams. I graduated from Saint Catherine's High School in Racine, Wis. A couple of years later, he was coming home late after a school event. In the fog, he hit and killed a former student. She was high on drugs and walking in the road. Audrey and I were married two years later. It was a foggy night and coach didn't make the 120-mile trip to our wedding because of the fog.

The second was a teacher at Loras College, who lived in Wisconsin. He used to give me rides when I was dating Audrey, a UW-Platteville student. He has since died, but he was a wonderful man who loved young people. One night coming home late in the fog, he hit and killed a drunk walking on the highway.

Two irresponsible people lost their lives and created a lot of pain for these two friends and their loved ones.

Some of the most difficult driving is in fog. Visibility is sometimes almost zero. This gives you and others little reaction time. Always drive with your dim headlights on. You will be able to see better, because your bright headlights reflect and make it even more difficult to see. This also makes it easier for other road users to see your vehicle. The white fog line on the right edge of the road will help you navigate, keeping you from driving over the center line or onto the shoulder.

Animals

Merlyn in gone now. He was my friend and mentor for more than 30 years. At one time he was a school administrator, a take-charge guy who was fussy about his clothes and his hair.

His custom was to drive around town with Charlie, his miniature Yorky, on his left shoulder. During the Christmas season, their family tradition was to always have chocolate-covered cherries at home.

One frigid December night, Merlyn returned frustrated from a difficult school board meeting. Being the go-getter type, he never enjoyed sitting and having to answer to, as he put it, "My five thousand bosses." Normally he was kind and compassionate, but Merlyn began to tease his little buddy. He would take a candy, wave it in front of the dog's nose, and plop it into his own mouth. His wife, Ann, and daughter Deedee told him he was being sadistic and should stop. This comment and Charlie's growling encouraged Merlyn to continue. Soon Charlie was sitting in his customary spot on Merlyn's shoulder, lifted his leg, and peed all over Merlyn's head. He bellowed for help to no avail. Ann and Deedee were on the floor in hysterics.

One gorgeous day my brother Mike was out riding motorcycles with a couple of friends. Creighton, in the lead, had a long flowing ponytail. During the drive, unbeknown to him, he was being hunted. A turkey vulture above thought his length of hair was a succulent squirrel. The bird descended, and 10 feet before seizing its prey, realized it wasn't a critter sitting atop Creighton's head. It decided to fly away.

Maybe you saw or heard the story about the lady in Iowa. She wrote the Des Moines Register and called WHO radio complaining about the Iowa DOT. She said they were placing deer crossing signs in the worst locations. The agency should have been selecting safer places for the deer to cross.

Curt, a friend from Winona, Minn., was an over-the-road trucker. He said he would hit a couple of deer a year. Sometimes they would be lodged up under the tractor when he returned home. The shop mechanics were never happy when this happened.

Over a five-year period I had four deer crashes, and Audrey had one. All of them did major damage to our vehicles. Two of mine were less than five months apart, October and March.

Both were on Old Highway 61, on a Thursday morning at 6 a.m. when I was on my way to Bible study. Maybe I should have prayed before I left home. With disease and increased hunting in Iowa, the deer population is down. I am not disappointed.

When you live in rural America, road kill lying in or alongside the road is common. These are animals hit by vehicles while trying to cross the highway. This June we saw a dead doe on the gravel shoulder near the Wapsipinicon River between Wheatland and Calamus. Next we saw two baby white-tailed deer not more than 18 inches high walking next to the road. They were a pretty brown with cute spots on their backs. When wild animals are hungry, they are not nearly as timid.

For some reason I lost the word fawn. I asked my students what a baby deer was called. Joe, my driver, was certain they were called Bambi. "No, that was the name of a Disney movie made about 80 years ago," I replied. Becca in the back seat remembered that "fawn" was the correct name.

Other animals besides deer that could be in the roadway are numerous. About 25 years ago Maggie and Jeff were driving in rural Milwaukee and saw a snapping turtle in the road. It measured almost three feet across. This caused an accident and traffic back-up.

One time Audrey came across a big snapping turtle and noticed a couple of guys in pickup trucks stop and fight over it. I have never tasted turtle myself so I can't say for sure if they have seven flavors of meat.

One time Audrey came across a big snapping turtle and noticed a couple of guys in pickup trucks stop and fight over it. I have never tasted turtle myself so I can't say for sure if they have seven flavors of meat.

Another friend totaled his car when he met a herd of cattle on Interstate 80.

On one of Sarah's drives this spring her Dad accompanied us. He told four driving stories. The first happened when Sarah was a baby.

Bob was driving west on Summit Street. There was a baby robin in the road by the high school football field. As he approached a hungry crow was after the helpless creature. Not liking these predators, Bob sped up. The crow disappeared and in the mirror he could see the young bird managed to hop back onto the grass.

When he got home, Bob pushed the button to open the garage door. Getting out, he looked at his grill, noticing a couple of black feathers. On his knees, he stuck his head under the radiator. The angry bird, still alive, stuck his beak out, almost hitting Bob's face.

The crow was angry and came after him. He reached inside his garage and grabbed a baseball bat to protect himself. Swinging at his attacker, he made contact, launching the little predator into the garage. It landed in Sarah's stroller where it hemorrhaged and died. Bob's wife was not very happy when she discovered the mess the crow made of the baby carriage.

Bob told another story about his other daughter, a student at the University of Iowa. At a light she got rear-ended. To avoid another crash, the man told her to pull into the parking lot on the corner so they could get each other's information. She pulled in and the guy took off. She should have taken a picture of the guy's license plate with her phone.

Once on Main Street in Maquoketa, Bob was waiting to pull from the curb. Up the block a person was trying to do a parallel park. After sideswiping the car ahead they took off. Bill wrote down the license number of the fleeing car. He put it under the windshield wiper of the damaged car, including his name and number. The people later called and thanked him for his kindness.

Bob's niece had a crash with her little brother in the car. He is now 21 years old and still afraid to get a driver's license.

Last spring we were driving on a country road. A field mouse crossed the road in front of our driver's ed car. From above and to our left a hawk descended on the mouse as we approached. We hit and killed the hawk. Looking in the mirror, I saw the mouse escape across the road unscathed.

We live on a frontage road next to Highway 61, a multi-lane highway. Roy was our next-door neighbor for 15 years. His feeder calves used to escape from their fenced-in lot. They preferred the fresh grass of our lawn and ditches to baled hay. Passers-by would get excited about his livestock near the road and call the sheriff's department. We used to be visited frequently by deputies only to say the cattle weren't ours.

Roy's cow and 400-pound calf disappeared. He had the pair pasturing at Jimmy's farm about six miles away.

A couple of weeks ago Roy went to bring the cattle home. Jimmy wasn't there but had his brother Rick help load them up. Apparently Rick didn't get the instructions to close the back gate of the trailer.

Roy is always in a hurry; he had chores to do and day-old bread to pick up from the Quad-Cities. You have probably heard it said that sometimes we don't have time to do it right, but we always have time to do it over. Often that is Roy's story.

Arriving home a few minutes later, Roy discovered he had no passengers. Because Jimmy's is the closest farm with livestock, naturally the sheriff's office notified him almost immediately that there was a cow wandering around on the blacktop east of Welton.

He located the cow quickly, but the calf was hidden in the tall weeds by the fence-line several feet below the road. Roy, Jimmy, and Mitch, another neighbor, worked from 4:30 to 6 p.m. to corral the cow, without success.

With chores finished, they returned again at 9 p.m. after dark. This time they quickly located and caught the calf, but were unable to entice Momma into the trailer. She spent the next three hours eluding capture by running circles through the ditch, bean fields, and cornfields.

The next morning at 6 a.m., with both calf and cow hungry, Roy alone coaxed mother back into the trailer with her baby.

Because we live near The Mississippi River we see bald eagles all year long. I see them flying almost every day when driving with Bellevue and Maquoketa students. Occasionally we will spot them roosting, feeding on road kill in the ditches or on the roadside. I love seeing them fly when the sun is shining; it reflects off their head and tail. This make them look as though they glow.

My wife is from Wisconsin and her folks raised hogs. Once while we were visiting, one big sow got hit on the busy Highway 14 east of Janesville where they lived.

Usually they were able to get cattle or hogs corralled before they got to the road. You haven't lived until you have been out at midnight, looking for black Angus cattle in a dark August cornfield.

In January, a horse got spooked and broke a fence and backed up traffic on a busy interstate as it ran alongside the road in the same direction as traffic. In this case, a police car drove along with it until other officers could respond and surround the horse near a bridge. Its owner came with the horse trailer to take it back home. No harm done to horse or human.

Stacey was driving to Lost Nation. It was 3:40 p.m. At first I thought I saw a black dog on the road about a mile west of Elwood on Highway 136. We got closer and realized it was a tall, black, skinny, long hog. It was on the shoulder rooting in the gravel. We looked around and didn't see any livestock around this location.

We stopped at the gas station in Lost Nation, concerned about someone possibly hitting this pig. The lady working at the station said she came to work at 1 p.m. and it was there when she went by. She said the people who live at that farm have a menagerie of exotic animals and they have been known to get out. This made sense, because this wasn't your typical pig.

Michael, a farmer, was driving in Omaha behind an old Honda. He thought a dog was in the backseat. Once closer, he thought there were two dogs in the back seat. As he passed he realized they were goats. One was a billy. There was also a third goat in the front passenger seat. The windows were closed. He could only guess what it smelled like inside. Then he noticed the lady eating as she drove. This almost caused him to hurl his own lunch.

In Iowa, deer are the biggest and most common highway animal hazard. They tend to move at dusk and dawn and usually in groups. It is worst from October to December; it's their mating season and the bucks aren't as vigilant as usual. This is also harvest time; deer get spooked by farm equipment and will travel day or night.

Slow down when you see animal crossing signs, or an animal on or by the road. After dark you sometimes will see the reflection of their eyes first.

According to the National Highway Traffic Safety Administration, one million car accidents with deer each year kill 200 Americans and cause more than 10,000 personal injuries, with $1 billion dollars in vehicle damage.

The popular Public Service Announcement in Iowa is, "Don't swerve for deer." That slogan may save your life. Also be careful how hard you brake. You could prevent a rollover, head-on, or rear-end collision.

Winter Driving

In the mid-'70s two of my college classmates tried to drive from Sioux City to Dubuque, Iowa, in a blizzard. They were returning from Christmas break. Anxious family and friends tried to discourage their departure, without success. They were traveling a two-lane road, back before cell phones were invented. When Chuck and his friend never arrived at school, they were reported missing and the search was on. The car was in a ditch under a snowdrift. Unable to escape, they held each other's feet to keep warm. Fortunately, under the snow the vehicle and its occupants were somewhat insulated from the cold. Eventually someone spotted the antenna of the car protruding from the bank of snow. They were saved only feet from a farm drive after one-and-a-half days in good health.

Have you ever noticed when vehicles slide into the ditch, how many are SUVs or pickups. People who own sport utility vehicles often think four-wheel drives can speed on slippery roads without consequence. In bad weather, often these drivers travel about 10 mph faster than the rest of traffic and what is prudent. Pickup trucks have rear-wheel drive. Without enough weight over the back axle they don't have much traction, which causes them to slide more easily. If weather or road conditions are bad, slow down. Speed is the number one contributing factor to most road crashes.

Marcy got her school permit in February 2005, just after turning 15. The last snow of the winter was a half-inch in March.

On her way to school that day she went into the ditch, taking out two aged mailboxes. One belonged to a local farm chemical business. I told the people to replace the old rusted out boxes and I would pay for them. They didn't replace the mailboxes with the standard one they had before. They went and bought two top-of-the-line mailboxes and charged me $130.

I guess I should be thankful they didn't charge me labor. The crash was one mile from my home. The wrecker pulled the car 10 feet back onto the road. Then he brought it home, which cost another $100.

The moral of this story is, if you ever destroy two rural mailboxes, have your neighbor pull the car out of the ditch, saving you $100. Then replace the mailboxes yourself so someone won't steal another $130 from you by buying "Cadillac style" mailboxes.

Two months later Marcy was on her way to school again. She made a left turn east on to 11th Street, then signaled and moved into the right lane. A first-year teacher with a brand new Ford Focus must have thought she was turning. The teacher pulled out and totaled her car when she hit Marcy's old Grand Marquis. The young lady was in a panic. Marcy called me on the teacher's cell phone. I said to just call the police, they would handle it. The teacher must have been either pitied or beautiful. She never got a ticket. Thankfully, it was not Marcy's fault and she did not lose her driving privileges.

Four years ago Audrey almost took a dip in the Wapsipinicon River on her way to school. It was an icy day and it didn't make much difference what your speed. Coming off the bridge, she did a 360-degree spin. The car slid down the embankment up next to the fence that separates the river's backwater and the roadside ditch. I arrived about the same time as Fred, the wrecker owner. He surveyed the scene and proceeded to drive her Taurus up the slope through four inches of snow and back up onto the road, to everyone's amazement. It shouldn't have been a surprise. This is what he does for a living.

Audrey has always been a cautious driver, but now is more timid in bad weather than ever. For the next three years I chauffeured her to and from Davenport on bad winter days. It is a one-hour round trip.

On Dec. 15 there were two major pileups in Metro Milwaukee. One had 70 cars involved. The second was 50. My niece and her husband were in the middle of the second. They drove under a bridge. On the other side there was a complete white-out. People started hitting brakes on the cold slippery pavement. Tina and Clark were hit five times.

She said it was really scary, because they didn't know when or where the next slam was coming from. They waited in their car more than four hours. Emergency help was on the scene quickly, providing aid and calm to all, with instructions not to leave. The police were so overwhelmed they never did get a report written. Eventually all were shuttled to a local hotel where rides and proper attention could be given.

We were driving on a Saturday up Highway 52 from Bellevue to Dubuque. It's a scenic, windy, hilly road. Snow was blowing across the road from the south. Two miles farther the snow was blowing across from the north. Weatherman, how does that work? Maybe that would be easier to explain than predicting the forecast.

My son, Tyler, did a 360-degree spin on the cloverleaf outside DeWitt soon after getting his license at 16. That gave him enough of a scare that he behaved himself during the winter months. Too bad this timidity didn't carry over the rest of the year. I am not sure how he kept a license through his junior and senior years of high school.

We travel a lot and have been out on the highway when it wasn't safe. My trooper friend always asks my students, "Is there a vacation emergency?" Meaning, what is anyone doing out here in dangerous winter weather!

Today schools are more proactive when it comes to school closings and the safety of their students. If they know that bad weather will strike during the school day, they just cancel.

For years, the roads were the most dangerous whenever we had an early-out for bad weather. The Central office would announce a couple of hours before closing. It took that much time to arrange bus drivers and associated details. By the time we were actually dismissed, the ice had already struck, and the roads were the worst. I live next to Highway 61. It is a four-lane highway and gets the most attention with the plows and salt. I am sure glad I didn't have to drive back roads and gravel, which are sometimes closed for days.

Years ago with poorer quality cars and fuel, winter driving problems were common. Don, a fellow-driving teacher, tells this story from when he was a kid. His Dad's gas tank got low, causing the fuel line to freeze up. This means there was water in the gas. The unhappy mechanic made his way out to their stalled car that frigid night. After getting the car running, he told Don's father it is just as easy to keep the tank half full as half empty. For the rest of his life that was his motto to his children and grandkids. Good advice for all.

Another driving story isn't about driving cars, but still relates to the science of centrifugal force and how that relates to curves. One fall we had the good fortune of getting to see Governor Mike Huckabee live. In 2001 a group of governors were invited to Utah for a series of meetings. This was the year before that state hosted the Winter Olympic Games.

Included in this conference was "The Governors' Bobsled Race." Huckabee initially thought the competition was just named for the dignitaries present.

When he was assigned a 16-year old Junior Olympic bobsled coach, he understood that he was to be part of the festivities. He was terrified. He knew his life's experiences had not prepared him for any type of winter activity, much less bobsledding.

He grew up in Arkansas without cold or snow. Wind chill was only an abstract concept. He had never chipped ice off frozen car windows or helped free stuck vehicles from snowdrifts. He hadn't shoveled for hours or knocked giant icicles off the side of houses. He never sprayed ether into a carburetor on a frozen engine that preferred to sleep rather than start.

The Governor also missed out on fun games of hockey on the neighbor's pond, snowball fights, tobogganing and sledding. We kids of the north knew when it was time to head for home. That was when both your fingers and toes went numb. At home then you would soak them in cold water to bring them back to life before trying to heat them up.

Bobsleds travel at up to 93 mph, but Huckabee was not to worry, because amateurs only hit 75 mph. His training involved a mile-long climb up a slope with spikes on his shoes. His coach instructed him about proper procedures and the dangers at each bend in the course.

Just before the start of the race, he was told that the centrifugal force would pull the sled at each curve. He was to steer into each new curve, because by the time the sled reacted they would be entering the following curve in the opposite direction. He also was not to worry about anything behind, because ice behind you can't hurt you. He and his coach placed second. They finished behind Utah's governor, the host of this event.

Highway speed limits vary in each state. They are set based on what is a safe speed under perfect conditions. The basic speed law is the speed that is safe to drive for the situation. You can be ticketed for driving at the posted speed if it is not safe to do so.

Twenty-three percent of all crashes are weather-related. More than 6,000 people each year die in these collisions, with another 480,000 injured. Almost half of these crashes happen during rain, about 40 percent are snow- and ice-related, with three percent during foggy conditions.[33]

Chapter 10: Divine Intervention

Coincidence or Not?

About 15 years ago, the DeWitt driver's ed car's accelerator malfunctioned on the gravel road north of Calamus. Danny, a friend, was almost run off the road by the out-of-control red sedan.

When the vehicle reached the curve it didn't make the turn, it rolled into the creek and onto its top.

In his newly purchased leather boots, Danny rushed to aid the occupants. The front door wouldn't budge, but he was able to wrench open the back. He was able to get the teacher and students out unharmed.

The grandfather of the girl driving was so thankful he offered to pay for Danny's ruined water-soaked boots. He appreciated the offer, but declined. Though he may have saved their lives, Danny was disappointed he never got a thank you from the teacher.

Seven years ago we were driving from Lost Nation, Iowa, through Elwood on Highway 136 on our way to Maquoketa. For some reason on this day there was no instructor's mirror in the car. This was our second drive of six. Each student drives one hour on a two-hour drive.

Our driver, Taylor, had not had much experience, unusual for a farm kid. We had a semi truck following us for about five miles. Most of my attention was on Taylor; he was not very confident with the instructions I was giving.

Just after crossing a bridge, we were turning left onto the Airport Road. He was taking a lot longer making a simple turn than what was necessary or safe. All of a sudden we heard the roar of the semi, which lasted 4 or 5 seconds, as he passed us on our left. He was probably going 55 mph.

The semi driver was careless and driving down a slight hill too fast. Because of the bridge he had no shoulder to drive onto. He had three options. One: after crossing the bridge he could have rolled his truck into the right ditch, probably ending his life. Two: he could rear-end our car, probably killing all three of us. Three: pass us and pray to God that Taylor continued to be indecisive a few moments longer. God must have been with us just then.

If we had turned a second or two sooner, the folks of Maquoketa would have had three lives to mourn that day. It took a few minutes before I understood the near-tragedy. I had a driver's instructor's mirror ordered online the very next day. I have never taught again without a teacher's mirror.

The lesson here is, when driving always pay attention, be respectful and patient with other drivers, especially when the car has a big sign on it that says STUDENT DRIVER.

In October on our last drive of the day, returning from Muscatine, Iowa, we were heading east on Interstate 80 going 63 mph approaching the Brady Street entrance ramp. With the cloverleaf's tight curve, 40-45 mph is the safe speed for most people entering the expressway. Our car was leading a pack of faster drivers working their way around us.

A black midsized car came off the cloverleaf from the north. This 60-something driver was going close to 60 mph, making it more difficult for all of us to adjust. He never looked over his left shoulder to check the lanes.

Fortunately, the cars behind were watching and had already backed off. Inches from colliding, I stomped my teacher brake. I am not sure that would have saved us. When Trae, our driver, realized what was happening, he jerked our car into the left lane without looking.

With all the traffic, it was a miracle we weren't hit from the right, rear, and left. Any of these scenarios would have caused an eight-car pile up. When we were able to move back to the right lane, the pack realized a calamity had been avoided. It only took seconds for them to proceed past us.

Our back-seat passenger said this blind man who almost caused a tragedy never even reacted. He had no clue what almost happened. My first question was, "How did this person live to be this old?"

Not a driving story but more divine intervention: Another time Mark, who was a teacher and coach, had the most successful softball program in the school's history. Some unhappy parents pressured the administration, and he lost his job. When he received the call that he had been fired from coaching the sport he loved, Mark was crushed.

Upset, he didn't want to say to his wife anything he might regret. He told her he was going to take a walk to the edge of town; he needed to think. For him this was a spiritual moment. He asked God for a sign that all would work out and this was meant to be.

Just a few moments later, a car drove up on this quiet country road and a young woman got out. She said that when she saw him, she knew she had to stop and let him know he was the best coach she had ever had through her competitive years. There it was, the sign that all was going to work out!

He was academically the best student in my class. Mason had a great attitude and was a very responsible teenage driver. His driving instructor had many years of teaching experience.

The side mirrors on his driver education car may have not been set correctly. Earlier, I explained how to properly set the mirrors in a car. They should be set to view out away from the rear panels. This is the proper procedure recommended by the Iowa DOT.

Mason was driving on Interstate 80. With abundant truck traffic, this at times is a dangerous expressway. His teacher wanted Mason in the safer right lane.

He told him to increase his speed, look, and move to the right. Not looking or speeding up, Mason didn't see the semi at his back right bumper. The instant he made his move to the right, the car was destroyed by the tractor-trailer. Fortunately, none of the three frightened occupants were injured.

Even though Mason didn't make a proper shoulder check, he should have been able to avoid this crash if the mirrors had been set properly.

Our driver education cars come equipped with teacher's dual brake and mirror. These are designed to keep the student driver and passengers safer. Even with these improvements, and 10 years of experience, I am a believer in divine intervention.

References

[1]"Top Party Schools in the US for 2015, 2014, 2013, and 2012." n.d. Princeton Review. www.collegeatlas.org/top-party-schools.html. Accessed April 15, 2015.

[2]"Is It Time To Ban Drivers' Licenses for 14-year-olds?" USA Today, June 6, 2012. http://content.usatoday.com/communities/driveon/post/2012/06/is-it-time-to-ban-drivers-licenses-for-14-year-olds/1#.VUefqCh7nQc. Accessed May 5, 2015.

[3]"Americans Adopt The Auto." The National Museum of American History. http://amhistory.si.edu./onthemove/exhibition_8_2.html. Accessed December 6, 2014.

[4]"Teen Drivers – Graduated Driver Licensing." National Highway Traffic Safety Administration. www.nhtsa.gov/Driving+Safety/Teen+Drivers/Teen+Drivers+Education/Teen+Drivers+-+Graduated+Driver+License. Accessed April 22, 2015.

[5]"Teen Crash Facts." Iowa Department of Transportation, January 31, 2008, page 10. www.iowadot.gov/mvd/ods/researchfacts.pdf. Accessed May 8, 2015.

[6]"Teen Crash Facts." Iowa Department of Transportation, January 31, 2008, page 10. www.iowadot.gov/mvd/ods/researchfacts.pdf. Accessed May 8, 2015.

[7]"Driving Deaths Due To Cell Phone Use Underreported: Study." NYDailynews.com. www.nydailynews.com/autos/cell-phone-driving-deaths-underreported-study-article-1.1337271. Accessed April 22, 2015.

[8]"Table 1103. Motor Accidents-Number and Deaths." U.S. Census Bureau, Statistical Abstract of the United States 2012. www.census.gov/compendia/statab/2012tables/1251103.pdf. Accessed December 17, 2014.

[9]"Because Texting and Driving Kills!" TextingandDrivingSafety.com. www.textinganddriving.com. Accessed May 4, 2015.

[10]Kotz, Deborah, "Driving Drowsy as Bad as Driving Drunk." U.S. News & World Report, November 8, 2010. http://health.usnews.com/health-news/family-health/sleep/articles/2010/11/08/driving-drowsy-as-bad-as-driving-drunk. Accessed May 7, 2015.

[11]"Connecticut Enacts First Speed–Limit Law." History.com. www.history.com/this-day-in-history/connecticut-enacts-first-speed-limit-law. Accessed December 4, 2015.

[12]"Americans Adopt the Auto." America On The Move. http://amhistory.si.edu/onthemove/exhibition/exhibion-8-7.htlm. Accessed May 5, 2015.

[13]"Connecticut Enacts First Speed – Limit Law." History. http://www.history.com/this-day-in-history/connecticut-enacts-firstspeed-limit-law. Accessed December 4, 2014.

[14]Looking Behind Us... The History of The Rear View Mirror." Snuggle Nugget. January 2, 2009. http://snugglenugget.wordpress.com. Accessed December 9, 2014.

[15]"Teen Crash Facts." Iowa Department of Transportation, January 31, 2008, page 18. www.iowadot.gov/mvd/ods/researchfacts.pdf. Accessed May 8, 2015.

[16]"The History of Seat Belts." About.com. http://theinventors.org/library/inventors/bl-seat-belts.htm. Accessed May 5, 2015.

[17]Bellis, Mary. "The History of Airbags." About.com. 2014. http://inventors.about.com/od/astartinventions/a/air_bag.html. Accessed December 4, 2014.

[18]"Iowa Seat Belt Use Survey 2014 Data Collection Methodology Report." Survey & Behavior Research Service, September 25, 2014, page 7. http://www.iowadot.gov/mvd/ods/stats/survey14.pdf. Accessed May 5, 2015.

[19]"Teen Crash Facts." Iowa Department of Transportation, January 31, 2008, page 18. www.iowadot.gov/mvd/ods/researchfacts.pdf. Accessed May 8, 2015.

[20]Hanson, David J. Ph,D. "Candace Lightner." Bio A&E Television Networks 2014. http://www.biography.com/people/candy-lightner-21173669. Accessed December 11, 2014.

[21]"2011 Drunk Driving Statistics." 2014 Alcohol Alert.com. 2014. http://www.alcoholalert.com/drunk-driving-statistics.html. Accessed December 6, 2014.

[22]Handfield, Rob. "A Brief History of the Highway Transportation System in the U.S." The SCRC ARTICLES LIBRARY, July 5, 2006. http://scm.ncsu.edu/scm-articles/article/a-brief-history-of-the-highway-transportation-system-in-the-U.S. Accessed December 3, 2014.

[23]"2012 Traffic Safety Facts Sheet." Rural/Urban Comparison." DOT HS 812050 NHTSA National Highway Traffic Safety Administration. www.nhtsa.gov/NCSA. Accessed December 3, 2014.

[24]"History of the Stop Sign." My Parking Sign. www.myparkingsign.com/MPS/article_History-of-stop-sign.aspx. Accessed April 24, 2015.

[25]"Intersection Safety." U.S. Department of Transportation Federal Highway Administration, slide 6. http://safety.fhwa.dot.gov/intersection/resources/intsafpst092609/long/. Accessed April 28, 2015.

[26]"Americans Adopt the Auto." America On The Move. http://amhistory.si.edu/onthemove/exhibition/exhibion-8-7.html. Accessed May 5, 2015.

[27]Mancone, Mary. "The History of Bicycles: An Abridged Time." Bicycles How-to. 2008. http://iml.jou.ufl.edu/projects/Fall08/Mancone/history.html. Accessed May 7, 2015.

[28]"Bicycles." National Highway Traffic Safety Administration. http://www.nhtsa.gov/Bicycles. Accessed May 7, 2015.

[29]"Bicycles and Other Cyclists." National Highway Traffic Safety Administration, April 2014. http://www-nrd.nhtsa.dot.gov/Pubs/812018.pdf. Accessed May 7, 2015.

[30]"Suzuke Hayabusa the Fastest Crotch Rocket in the World." Crotch Rocket Guide. http://www.crotchrocketguide.com/suzuki-hayabusa-the-fastest-crotch-rocket-in-the-world/. Accessed May 7, 2015.

[31]"Motorcycle Fact Sheet." Governor's Traffic Safety Bureau Iowa Department of Public Safety, October 2012. http://www.dps.state.ia.us/commis/gtsb/pdfs/motorcycle_fact_sheet.pdf. Accessed May 8, 2012.

[32]"Stay Alert, Stay Alive!" Iowa Department of Transportation Iowa Motorcycle Operator Manual. http://www.iowadot.gov/mvd/ods/mcmanual. Accessed May 11, 2015.

[33]"How Do Weather Events Impact Roads?" Department of Transportation Federal Highway Administration. February 25, 2014. http://www.ops.fhwa.dot.gov/weather/gl_roadimpact.htm. Accessed December 15, 2014.